Zen Anarchism
The Egalitarian Dharma of Uchiyama Gudō

Contemporary Issues in Buddhist Studies

Series Editor, Richard K. Payne

Zen Anarchism
The Egalitarian Dharma of Uchiyama Gudō

Fabio Rambelli

Institute of Buddhist Studies and
BDK America, Inc.
2013

First Printing, 2013
ISBN: 978-1-886439-51-1
Library of Congress Catalog Card Number: 2013942778

Published by
Institute of Buddhist Studies and BDK America, Inc.
2620 Warring Street
Berkeley, California 94704

Printed in the United States of America

Contents

Contents

Foreword

Richard K. Payne

These essays from the *fin de siècle* Japanese Zen priest Uchiyama Gudō—collected, translated, and introduced by Fabio Rambelli—introduce us to an otherwise little-known aspect of Buddhist history: the relations that can be constructed between the buddhadharma and radical political critique and action. The importance of these works reaches beyond the history of Buddhism in modern Japan to deepen our appreciation of the complexity of the tradition as a source for resisting modernity's seemingly ever more pervasive forms of social control.

Buddhist complicity with the imperial authorities in the first half of the twentieth century, both within Japan and in the "Greater East Asia Co-Prosperity Sphere" (Dai-tō-a Kyōeiken 大東亜共栄圏), has come under increasing scrutiny as a subject of scholarly attention, adding an important perspective to our understanding of the modern social history of Buddhism. For those of us who came of "religious age" in the 1960s and 70s, this has meant abandoning idealized images of Buddhist culture in Japan as one solely of serene gardens, genteel tea ceremonies, and haiku. No doubt we could have more fully recognized the contradictions between protesting the Vietnam War and D. T. Suzuki's essays on Zen and *bushidō* (the "way of the warrior"). Rambelli shows us that beyond complicity and Romanticized idealization, our understanding of Buddhist history in modern Japan must be broadened to include a third option—that of resistance. In the adaptation of Buddhism to the present day, Uchiyama's vision of Buddhism as a powerful tool of social critique may serve to confront the conformism, complacent self-satisfaction, and narcissism of the consumerist appropriation of Buddhism as yet another commodity in the religio-therapeutic marketplace.

I wish to express my thanks to Fabio Rambelli for his good humor and friendship; to Sallie B. King for her Introduction, exploring the relevance of Uchiyama for contemporary Engaged Buddhism; to Marianne Dresser for her editorial and layout work; to Yufuko Kurioka for assistance with the always complex issue of proper transcription of Japanese names; to Cynthia Col for the index; and to Arlene Kato for the cover design. As always, deep bows of appreciation go to Rev. Brian Nagata and BDK America for their interest and support, and to the members of the Buddhist Churches of America, especially the Fraternal Benefit Association whose Legacy Fund supports the publication of this series.

Preface

Fabio Rambelli

Buddhism is not commonly associated with radical and revolutionary politics. A notable exception is a political science fiction novel by Riccardo Pedrini, a member of the Italian writers' collective known as Wu Ming. The novel imagines Italy being ruled in the near future by a government that upholds a strange ideological combination of Theravāda Buddhism and Antonio Negri's radical thought.[1] This novel contains important political statements, including the idea that the current political system can only be replaced by a kind of utopia (though this utopia is itself deeply flawed, as it cannot fulfill its initial promise of liberation). Almost a century before this novel was written, the Japanese Zen monk Uchiyama Gudō, attempting an analogous junction between Mahayana (Zen) Buddhism and anarchist radical thought, employed an intellectual mix that also included late-Romantic themes, Christian images, and references to the Japanese tradition of righteous (and self-defeating) revolt.

This book focuses on the writings and activities of Uchiyama Gudō (1874–1911), a Sōtō Zen priest and socialist-anarchist activist. Gudō was ordained in 1897, and in 1904 he became the resident priest of Rinsenji, a small mountain temple in the Hakone area near Mt. Fuji, not far from Tokyo. From around that time, he became painfully aware of the wretched conditions of dispossessed peasants and joined the Japanese socialist movement. He explicitly claimed that a Buddhist perspective was the starting point for his allegiance to socialism.

He later joined author and revolutionary activist Kōtoku Shūsui (1871–1911) in the Japanese anarchist movement. Gudō started a clandestine press in his temple and printed a few anarchist communist publications, one of which he wrote while the others were written by representatives of European anarchism. After several vicissitudes, Gudō was arrested for his alleged involvement in a terrorist plot to assassinate the emperor (known as the "High Treason Incident," *taigyaku jiken*) in 1910, and after a rigged trial he was sentenced to death in 1911. He left two incomplete manuscripts, written in prison, about his political and social ideals.

Anarchism in Japan received a mortal blow with the High Treason Trial and the death sentences meted out to its most influential members, although it continued to play a role in politics and society until the 1920s. The apogee of the international anarchist movement ended with the defeat of its political organizations during the Spanish Civil War in 1936–1939.[2] After that, world anarchism became more and more marginalized.

From the extant material on Uchiyama Gudō we get a glimpse of an extended network of provincial intellectuals from the rising middle class who were steeped in traditional Japanese thought (Buddhism, Confucianism) but at the same time open to new ideas from the West.[3] Christianity was a very influential intellectual system at the time, but other ideas were circulating as well. Anarchism, in particular, constituted an influential global discourse, with texts, ideas, and people circulating between Europe, the Americas, and Asia.[4]

Gudō and his group of fellow intellectuals were attracted not by the ideas favored by the establishment, but rather by radical ideologies of freedom, social equality, and happiness. Though it may seem strange to us, reading their works a hundred years later, individual happiness was one of the central keywords as well as one of the main goals of anarchism, even for its Japanese epigones. Most of all, these intellectuals were painfully aware of the growing disparity of wealth and opportunities in contemporary Japanese society, and they tried to find ways to counter the processes causing such disparity through political action. They were not only free thinkers but also engaged individuals. Several, including Gudō, forfeited their lives for their ideas.

A micro-historical look at one of these individuals, Uchiyama Gudō, offers insight into this previously neglected network of people and ideas. Their difficult attempts to bring together traditional thought (in Gudō's case, Buddhism) and new revolutionary attitudes—not only in politics, but also in social customs and practices—was a very innovative and potentially also very productive mix. Regrettably, state repression destroyed these possibilities before they could develop into full-fledged political and cultural alternatives.

However, we cannot fail to notice that Gudō's three main ideas, namely, rejection of the divine nature of emperor, liberation of tenant farmers, and abolition of military conscription, were all achieved after the end of World War II. Specifically, these changes came about with the Emperor's Declaration of Humanity (*ningen sengen*) of 1945 and the dismantling of State Shinto following the Shinto Directive of 1945, the agrarian reform of 1947 that effectively ended exploitation by big landowners and gave land to those who cultivate it, and the abolition of the Japanese army formally sanctioned by the Constitution of Japan. Thus, ideas that were highly revolutionary—indeed, deemed treasonous—in Gudō's time became standard policy less than forty years later.

The rapidity of these changes is an indication of the extent of sociopolitical transformation that has taken place in Japan over the past few decades. It should be noted, however, that these momentous changes took place under the Allied Occupation following the defeat of imperial Japan in World War II and were not necessarily the result of internal social movements.

In addition, other goals of the early anarchist revolutionary movement are also now standard policies in Japan. These include women's autonomy and legal equality, a welfare system (including health coverage and pensions), free education, and a high degree of wealth redistribution. Postwar Japan has also developed many forms of public meetings, which take place at apartment complexes, in neighborhoods (*chōnaikai*), at schools, and in municipal assemblies, something that Gudō, with his fervent belief in the power of people's self-organization and self-decision, might have appreciated.[5] One might imagine that if many people attended these meetings, which are largely consultative in nature, they might also have a chance to influence actual policy-making processes. But Gudō may have been unpleasantly surprised by how few people actually attend such meetings and how few discussions of policies (and politics) actually take place. It is as if, when given the chance to govern themselves, people chose to delegate all decision-making to authorities. Could Gudō have imagined at least in part such an outcome when he supposedly revealed to the investigators his doubts about the anarchical system?[6]

In spite of this, the actuality and relevance today of at least some of Gudō's concerns is uncanny: unbridled, exploitative financial capitalism; important decisions made unilaterally, without extensive discussion involving many citizens; reduced opportunities of social improvement for many young people; the need to develop local systems of production and distribution (instead of depending on imports from distant places)—all are items on the agenda of any serious, progressive political program today.[7] In any case, the question concerning the actual contribution of the modern socialist/anarchist movements to Japanese society remains. Part of the problem is that accounts of Japanese society tend to reflect the dominant ideologies of the establishment and the ruling elites, and therefore downplay or ignore alternative visions and practices, or, if they do take them into account, tend to treat them as aspects of "subculture."

It is quite possible that the consensus-oriented aspects of Japan are the result not only of a paternalistic but essentially authoritarian tradition, but also of more democratic forms of government—perhaps, ultimately based on Buddhist thought and Buddhist forms of governance. In the large Buddhist monastic organizations in East Asia, with their long history of communitarian life and action, their sense of autonomy and independence, and their political traditions of self-rule (which, in some cases at least, were explicitly democratic in nature[8]) Gudō clearly saw a model for a modern socialist/anarchist society.

Interestingly, no one in Japan since Gudō has pursued this possibility in an explicit or systematic manner. What has instead happened is the fragmentation of Buddhist organizations into small, family-managed temple units and, at the level of institutional sectarian organizations, a continuation of discourses and rituals that are largely disconnected from contemporary society.

Still open to discussion are the possible reasons for the substantial lack of Buddhist contributions to progressive political and social movements in Japan, and, more generally, the potential to form explicitly progressive, political stances of a clear Buddhist orientation in the modern world. In recent years, we have seen large Buddhist mobilizations against state repression in Burma (Myanmar) and Tibet, but these fledgling movements lacked political organization and were not able to formulate clear political alternatives.

At the same time, a conservative (if not outright reactionary) drift has affected several political organizations in Asia that define themselves as "Buddhist." For instance, the Japanese political party Kōmeitō has moved steadily toward the conservative bloc; Sri Lankan left-wing Buddhist organizations have become staunchly nationalistic and in favor of military intervention against the Tamil minority; and, more recently, Buddhist organizations in southern Thailand are engaging in violent means against the large Muslim minority in those areas.[9]

The various forms of so-called "engaged Buddhism," which base their social activism on more or less explicit Buddhist values, seem often to lack both solid roots in classical Buddhist visions of politics and society and strong connections to modern liberation traditions. In this respect, the time has come for a thorough investigation of neglected but multifarious and influential forms of egalitarian traditions in premodern Asia, including those that developed from within Buddhism.[10]

In this book, I present a critical discussion of Gudō's texts and the complex and conflicting relationships between Buddhist teachings and anarchism in his thought and practice. Until now, authors have considered these texts as almost self-explanatory, and Gudō's anarchism has been described as only superficially related to Buddhist politics and ethics. In contrast, I place Gudō's writings within their plural cultural and historical contexts: in particular, Buddhist thought, socialist thought and praxis (which, in Japan and elsewhere, also included Christian elements), and the Edo-period Japanese tradition of anti-authoritarian political activism—which drew, among other sources, from Daoist elements and the thought of Wang Yangming.

The book is divided into two parts with an appendix. Part One is a critical account of Uchiyama Gudō's thought; Part Two contains translations of all of Gudō's major works. Chapter One presents a short intellectual biography of Gudō with descriptions of his works. Chapter Two is a detailed account of his thought, with special focus on its Buddhist foundations and their connections with socialism and especially anarchism as he envisioned them. I pay particular attention to the religious components of Gudō's political thought, including his stunning description of the spirit of freedom animating human beings, which he envisioned, literally, as a "mysterious holy spirit" (*fukashigi no seirei*) circulating in the blood and transmitted from one generation to the next—a spirit that naturally leads humans to strive for a condition of maximum freedom, understood by Gudō as anarchist communism.

Chapter Three addresses the philosophical precedents and intellectual strategies of Gudō's thought. I show that Gudō, in a more or less conscious and explicit way, tried to combine revolutionary thought and praxis from the West (socialism first and anarchism later, but also aspects of Christianity) with precedents from the Japanese tradition (Buddhism, Daoism, Confucianism, even Shinto). This combination was not random or wholesale but involved a high degree of critical acumen that brought Gudō to reject the more authoritarian moral elements of Confucianism and State Shinto, and the Christian propensity for miracles, and instead emphasize the revolutionary and liberative potential in the various traditions.

Part Two presents annotated translations of Gudō's most representative writings, including the translations of two anarchist articles he published, his printed pamphlet *Museifu kyōsan kakumei* ("Anarchist Communist Revolution"), and the posthumous manuscripts *Heibon no jikaku* ("Common Consciousness") and the so-called *Gokuchū shuki* ("Fragment from a Prison Manuscript"). The Appendix contains the original texts of the anarchist articles that Gudō's associates translated into Japanese and

Gudō printed in his clandestine press and circulated: the anonymous *"Aux conscripts"* (here in English translation from the French original) and Max Baginski's "Anti-Moral Considerations."

Overall, in this book I raise the issue of the place of Uchiyama Gudō's thought—and, in general, of Japanese democratic and libertarian tradition—in Japanese society. I envision this, in a much broader perspective, as a step toward reconceptualizing received views on "traditional Asian values" as essentially authoritarian and conservative, and the possibility of a progressive political agenda explicitly based on classical Buddhist thought.

Only a few works on Uchiyama Gudō exist in Japanese, notably, Kashiwagi Ryūhō's *Uchiyama Gudō: Taigyaku jiken no ideorōgu* (Toki, Japan: Kaiko no sha, 1976), and *Taigyaku jiken to Uchiyama Gudō* (Tokyo: JCA shuppan, 1979); and Morinaga Eizaburō's *Uchiyama Gudō* (Tokyo: Ronsōsha, 1984), of which the latter is the most complete study of Gudō's life and thought. These works also include various materials written by Gudō, including his own texts, the translations he published, personal letters, and excerpts from his contributions to the magazine *Heimin shinbun* and from documents related to the High Treason trial. In addition, significant portions of the following works are dedicated to Gudō: Inagaki Masami, *Henkaku wo motometa bukkyōsha* (Tokyo: Daizō shuppan, 1975); Yoshida Kyūichi, *Nihon kindai bukkyō shakaishi kenkyū*, 2 vols., in *Yoshida Kyūichi chosakushū*, vols. 5–6 (Tokyo: Kawashima shoten, 1991, rev. ed.) and *Nihon kindai bukkyōshi kenkyū*, in *Yoshida Kyūichi chosakushū*, vol. 1 (Tokyo: Kawashima shoten, 1992); Kihara Minoru, *Ryōka no nagare: Waga kusawake no shakaishugisha-tachi* (Tokyo: Orijin shuppan sentā, 1977); and Sueki Fumihiko, *Meiji shisōka ron* (Kindai Nihon no shisō saikō, vol. 1) (Tokyo: Toransubyū, 2004), pp. 241–266. Gudō's main works are also included in "Uchiyama Gudō shū," in *Sōtō shū sensho*, vol. 6 (Kyoto: Dōhōsha shuppan, 1982), pp. 245–292.

To date, the only discussions of Gudō in English are in Brian Victoria, *Zen at War* (New York and Tokyo: Weatherhill, 1996), pp. 38–48; Ishikawa Rikizan, "The Social Response of Buddhists to the Modernization of Japan: The Contrasting Lives of Two Sōtō Zen Monks," *Japanese Journal of Religious Studies* 25 (1–2) (1998): 87–115, especially pp. 98–104; and my own essay, "'The Dharma Preaches Equality and Has No Hierarchy': Buddhism and the Anarcho-Communist Movement in Japan," in Patrice Ladwig, ed., *Buddhist Socialisms in Asia* (London and New York: Routledge, forthcoming).

Acknowledgments

This project began as a sort of self-challenge for me as an attempt to move away from the history of medieval Japanese religion toward more "contemporary" topics, and indeed this is the first work I publish dealing with a twentieth-century subject. It is also a manifestation of my long-standing interest in Buddhist political thought and praxis on the one hand, and on Japanese attempts to integrate different intellectual systems on the other. I am sure I have not been able to overcome my obvious limitations as a dilettante in modern Japanese Buddhism, but I do hope that the understanding I present in this book—Uchiyama Gudō not as a heroic but hapless provincial monk, but as a creative intellectual trying to come to terms with both new discourses (socialism first and anarchism later) and his own cultural tradition—will bring a fresh perspective not only on the subject but also on the interpretation of aspects of modern Buddhism in general.

I would like to express my gratitude to Patrice Ladwig, who gave me the idea to write on Uchiyama Gudō; Nadine Willems and Sabine Frühstück for their important comments; Emily Simpsons for her accurate reading and Marianne Dresser for her fine editorial work; Cynthia Col and Yufuko Kurioka for their work on the index; and Silvio Vita, Watanabe Minoru (of Sapporo University Library), Sugamoto Yasuyuki, James Mark Shields, Or Porath, Geoff Evans, and my students in the Buddhist Politics seminar at the University of California, Santa Barbara, in 2011. I am very grateful to Sallie King for her insightful preface to this volume. Finally, many thanks to Richard Payne for accepting this monograph in the Contemporary Issues in Buddhist Studies Series.

Introduction:
Uchiyama Gudō and
Engaged Buddhism

Sallie B. King

Uchiyama Gudō courageously stood up to violent state oppression while struggling on behalf of the poor; his greatness lies in this. In recent decades, many members of the contemporary movement known as Engaged Buddhism have, like Gudō, championed the downtrodden while standing up in the face of extreme violence. Engaged Buddhism does not represent the entirety of contemporary Buddhist political engagement; there is very conservative and even militant political engagement by Buddhists as well. However, Gudō is much more akin to the progressive stance of the Engaged Buddhists. Therefore it may be instructive to look at Gudō and the Engaged Buddhists side by side to see what light may be shed on the larger pattern of twentieth- and twenty-first–century progressive Buddhist political engagement.

Engaged Buddhism is a contemporary form of Buddhism that engages with the political, social, and economic problems of society as a concrete expression of such core Buddhist values as compassion and nonviolence. It is nonsectarian and found throughout the Buddhist world. Quite a few of its leaders and activists have stood up to violence, sometimes in the form of violent state oppression, and/or have championed the downtrodden. The Burmese monks and nuns of the "Saffron Revolution" have challenged Burma's violent military dictatorship and promoted democracy and human rights with massive street demonstrations that led to arrests, torture and sometimes death for the monks and nuns. Dr. B. R. Ambedkar championed the untouchables of India, one of the most downtrodden people in the world, in the face of the severe oppression of societal caste-based real and potential violence. During the war in Vietnam, the monk-led "Struggle Movement" filled the streets, calling for an end to the war and succeeding in removing from office a succession of South Vietnamese governments they saw as intensifying the war that was killing so many of their countrymen;

again, many arrests, acts of torture, and deaths resulted. Tibetans in large numbers have struggled nonviolently against the overwhelming might of the occupying People's Republic of China, again with arrests, torture, and deaths.

Among Engaged Buddhist leaders, the Dalai Lama and Vietnamese monk Thich Nhat Hanh have suffered assassination attempts. Sri Lankan layman A. T. Ariyaratne and Indian layman B. R. Ambedkar continued their work while facing down very real death threats. Aung San Suu Kyi of Burma suffered personal attack and lived under house arrest for fifteen years. Thai layman Sulak Sivaraksa was twice charged and once imprisoned for *lèse-majesté*.[1]

In a time and place in which extremely few people dared to defy state power, Uchiyama Gudō worked within a very small and largely, by necessity, secret circle of like-minded activists, appealing in speech and writing to the impoverished peasants he championed but who were largely unresponsive. In a very different era, the Engaged Buddhist leaders have struggled against deadly state, and sometimes societal, power, but they did not and do not struggle alone; they have led mass movements in which hundreds of thousands of activists and supporters turned out in the streets. They often command global media coverage. The best known among them are famous, even celebrities, and heroes to millions.

Uchiyama Gudō and Engaged Buddhism are both products of modernity, specifically a defining characteristic of modernity: the belief that social and political institutions are the products of human beings, not inevitable, and very much open to correction and even fundamental change. There were of course multiple causes of differing fates of Gudō's and Engaged Buddhists' efforts, but among them we may cite their different historical placements. Gudō lived at the cusp of modernist ideology's entry into Japan. He passionately embraced ideas of socialism and anarchism that had recently arrived from the West, seeing them as practical methods of addressing the devastating poverty of the peasants among whom he lived, and feeling an intuitive kinship especially between Buddhism and socialism. However, the ideas he championed had by no means been assimilated yet by the Japanese peasants who, as Gudō noted, were "deeply traditionalist"; ideologically, he left those peasants far, far behind. In contrast, the Engaged Buddhists have worked in an Asia that has been very much changed by the forces of modernity. In this more recent era, when the Engaged Buddhist leadership invited them, the people readily flooded the streets, demanded their rights, and called for regime change.

How do the social and political views of Gudō and the Engaged Buddhists relate to their Buddhist commitments? There is no political or economic theory per se in the teachings of the Buddha. The Buddha accepted the political institutions of his time as givens. Over the centuries, moreover, Buddhist monks served as advisors to many governments, virtually all of them autocratic in nature. Gudō, however, was a committed socialist. Among Engaged Buddhist leaders and intellectuals also there is a strong tendency toward embracing socialist theory, as well as a striking aversion to capitalism. Many Asian Engaged Buddhist intellectuals and activists immediately and intuitively feel that capitalism is fundamentally incompatible with Buddhism. It is regarded as promoting greed, materialism, hedonism, and a spirit of grasping for one's own (or one's company's) good, heedless of the welfare of others or of society at large. Buddhism is seen as promoting moderation, contentment with what one has and a concern with the welfare of all, not only oneself or one's own family.

It is not only committed Buddhists who see things this way. Thai economists, who were aware that a growth economy requires consumerism, labeled Buddhism a regressive force with respect to the country's development, since Buddhism advocates contentment and moderation. The Thai government took this so much to heart that it forbade monks from teaching contentment, since it was inimical to economic growth. Thai "development monks" (who are Engaged Buddhists) responded by emphasizing such teachings all the more.

Beginning with economics, we note that both Gudō and a number of the Engaged Buddhists are seriously concerned with poverty. It seems clear that Gudō's strongest motivation for entering into political work is the poverty and suffering of the peasants around him. His work *Museifu kyōsan kakumei* ("Anarchist Communist Revolution") begins by asking, "Why is life so hard for tenant farmers?" It is addressed throughout to impoverished tenant farmers and urges them to rise up against those who oppress them. This concern for the poor is the driving force behind Gudō's brief revolutionary life.

Similarly, a number of the Engaged Buddhists take poverty as a primary concern. They point out that Buddhism itself is no friend of poverty. When the Buddha spoke to laypeople about economic matters, he taught them to follow right livelihood, which entailed not only earning one's livelihood in a moral and non-harmful way, but also earning enough to be able to support oneself and one's dependents, invest in one's business, give to holy men and beggars, and have some left over to

save against future need. He advised rulers that if they wanted to eliminate crime in their kingdoms they should eliminate poverty. On one occasion, often cited by the Engaged Buddhists, he refused to teach the
Dharma until a hungry man was fed.

Sri Lankan lay Engaged Buddhist leader A. T. Ariyaratne has spent
his life working to develop the impoverished villages of Sri Lanka. The
Sarvodaya Shramadana organization that he founded has helped thousands of villages improve their material condition by helping them or-
ganize themselves to build roads, wells, health clinics, and preschools
with their own hands, and helping the villagers to get training and
micro-loans to staff these institutions and start their own businesses.
Such a program would have been a dream come true for Gudō, had he
been able to bring it to the impoverished villagers of his Japanese parish.

What particularly exercises both Gudō and the Engaged Buddhists is
the disparity in wealth between the poor and the affluent. Gudō says to
the tenant farmers:

> You folks wake up early in the morning with the birds and work until dark,
> yet cannot get rid of poverty. . . . They wear silk kimonos without having to
> pick up even one single leaf of mulberry, and live in luxury drinking sake
> and eating meat as they please.

As for the Engaged Buddhists, upon hearing that the number of bil-
lionaires in America was growing, the Dalai Lama, usually so soft-spo-
ken, said:

> This I consider to be completely immoral. . . . While millions do not even
> have the basic necessities of life . . . the inequity of wealth distribution is a
> scandal.[2]

For his part, Ariyaratne developed a "Buddhist economics" that promotes a Middle Path society with "no poverty, no affluence" and "no
need, no greed." He stated that the superpowers "have no moral right to
spend $900 billion a year for armaments when 900 million people are
starving."[3] Thich Nhat Hanh made this into a precept, urging his fol-
lowers to take to heart: "Do not accumulate wealth while millions are
hungry."[4] There is no doubt that Gudō and the Engaged Buddhists see
eye to eye on this subject.

Interestingly, both Gudō and some of the Engaged Buddhists are will-
ing to challenge some basic, traditional Buddhist teachings in the interest of changing the lot of the poor and oppressed. Popular interpretations of karma are especially targeted. Gudō writes:

> You tenant farmers, you who produce food, . . . every year ends in scarcity for you. What sort of bad luck is this? Is it because of what the Buddhists call bad retribution from your past lives? But seriously, folks, if today, in our world in the twentieth century, you are still deceived by this kind of superstition, you will really end up like cows and horses.

What Gudō here refers to as "bad retribution from your past lives" is the traditional understanding of the Buddhist teaching of karma, the notion that things that happen to us in our present life were caused by our own actions in a past life. Thus, for example, being born into a lifetime of poverty is understood to be the result of one's own stinginess in a past life. The implication is that one has nothing to complain about; one's current suffering is the result of one's own actions and is therefore just.

Displaying a remarkably similar attitude, Sulak Sivaraksa calls "Establishment Buddhism" to task for its role in justifying fundamentally unjust social and economic situations. Pointing to the practice of Southeast Asian landlords charging peasants as much as 70 percent of the harvest for permission to farm the land, Sulak writes:

> Establishment Buddhism . . . explains this oppression as the working of karma, saying that both peasants and the landlord are reaping the results of their actions in former lives; the peasants of bad deeds and the landlord of merit achieved by building temples and images of the Buddha.[5]

Much as Marx saw religion as the "opiate of the masses," Gudō and Sulak are both keenly aware of the power of traditional teachings on karma to pacify an oppressed population into accepting an unjust situation against which, in their view, they should strenuously struggle. Whereas Gudō harshly dismisses this as "superstition," Sulak advocates its reinterpretation and recontextualization:

> Non-establishment buddhism, with a small b, is against this trend of wrong teaching. If the landlord understands and practices *dana* (generosity) he will know that it is wrong to take 70% of the harvest when the workers do not have enough to sustain them. . . . [A]t the same time, . . . out of *metta* (loving-kindness) and compassion people will share whatever extra they have. . . .[6]

In other words, it is "Establishment Buddhism" that is to blame— wealthy, heavily institutionalized Buddhism that is perhaps beholden to rich landowners for their substantial gifts to the temples. In Sulak's view, "small b" buddhism, which maintains true Buddhist values, tempers any inappropriate interpretations of karma by bringing considerations of generosity, loving-kindness, and compassion to the forefront of our thinking.

Turning to socialism, Gudō claimed that his embrace of socialism was based on his Buddhist values. When given the opportunity to state why he was a socialist, Gudō wrote:

> As a Buddhist preacher . . . these are the golden words that constitute the basis of my religious faith, namely, "All sentient beings have buddha-nature," "This Dharma is undifferentiated and there is no high and low in it," and "All sentient beings are my children." When I discovered that what socialism says is in perfect accord with these maxims, I became a believer . . . in socialism.

Here, Gudō shows that for him the connection between socialism and Buddhism was what he saw as Buddhism's teaching of human equality.

As Fabio Rambelli points out, the teachings cited by Gudō were not typically taken as affirmations of human equality in the Japanese Buddhism of the time. This is true. However, be that as it may, Gudō clearly took the teaching of buddha-nature and the teachings in the other passages as implying human equality. This is noteworthy, because the Engaged Buddhists also very much perceive Buddhist teachings, including those cited by Gudō, as affirming human equality. They emphasize that the Buddha taught all castes and both genders; put no class, caste, or gender restrictions on entry into the ordained sangha; and affirmed the enlightenment of members of all groups. The great ex-Untouchable leader B. R. Ambedkar converted from Hinduism and embraced Buddhism precisely because he saw the Buddha, in word and deed, as preaching human equality, and because he saw Buddhism as an apt vehicle for helping the ex-Untouchable class to realize their own equality and self-worth. Mahayana Engaged Buddhists, like Gudō, emphasize that all possess buddha-nature and are therefore equal.

Gudō was one of the earliest in what has become a long line of Buddhist intellectuals who see an inherent connection between Buddhism and socialism. The Engaged Buddhist tendency to embrace socialism was well articulated by the Thai monk Buddhadasa Bhikkhu, an advocate of what he called, "Dhammic Socialism." He sees socialism as the most natural and appropriate way of structuring human society, insofar as it replicates on a societal level the most fundamental law of the natural world, conditionality (Pāli *idappaccayata*). He explains this as follows:[7]

> In the teachings of the Buddha, everything arises as a consequence of other things. In the Buddha's words,

> When this exists, that comes to be; with the arising of this, that arises. When this does not exist, that does not come to be; with the cessation of this, that ceases.[8]

Thus all things exist in a state of profound dependence upon other things; this is conditionality. That is, all things exist within a great web of interdependence, in which all things both condition and are conditioned by other things. Thus, nothing exists or can exist for a moment in a state of solitariness or separation from other things. However, humankind's deep, subconscious view of the nature of reality is profoundly at odds with the true, interdependent nature of reality. Indeed, humankind's powerful intuitive sense that "I" am a "self" separate from the world and separate from other "selves" is, according to Buddhism, both profoundly mistaken and the source of everything that is wrong with us. Thus, the very focus of the teaching of the Buddha is the error of the gut-level belief that "I am" separate from all else and the focus of the practice he taught is the uprooting of this belief.

It is on the basis of these fundamental Buddhist teachings that Buddhadasa Bhikkhu writes:

> Dhammic Socialism according to Buddhist principles holds that Nature created beings which must live in groups. Both plants and animals live together in groups or communities. This system we will call "socialism": the correctness necessary for living together in groups which Nature has dictated. In short, it is living for the benefit of society, not for the individual benefit of each person.[9]

Thus, nothing in nature exists for a moment without other things: we all depend upon air, food, water, the beings that brought us into being, the microorganisms upon which all these beings depend, and so on. On a human societal level, we depend not only for our existence upon our parents and ancestors before them; in terms of the kind of being we are (trustful and outgoing, or fearful and reclusive; learned or ignorant, etc.) we also depend upon our parents' care or neglect, the childhood acquaintances who bullied or befriended us, our teachers' harshness or kindness, etc. If any of those factors, or many others, had been different, we would be different, not only in trivial ways but in our basic character or personality. This is how the law of conditionality (when this exists, that comes to be; when this does not exist, that does not come to be) plays out in human life.

Buddhadasa's point is that since this state of conditionality is the fundamental law of our being, we should live accordingly. This is what he calls "correctness": the correct behavior that follows naturally from the facts of reality. Socialism—"living for the benefit of society, not for the individual"—is, thus, the "correct" political system, since it is built upon the facts of reality: "I" would not be the individual that I am without society. The individual should recognize this and rather than selfishly attempting to maximize his or her own individual benefit, should strive to live in such a way that benefits the whole, society. Clearly, this social and political ideal aligns very neatly with the Buddhist ideal of existentially realizing selflessness and living a life of loving-kindness (*mettā*) and compassion (*karuṇā*) toward others. While this particular articulation is Buddhadasa's, this kind of thinking is very widespread among Engaged Buddhist intellectuals. It has made Engaged Buddhists tend to embrace socialism as a sociopolitical ideology that seems to be a natural expression of the Buddhist worldview and its spirituality.

This perceived natural, ideological fit between Buddhism and socialism notwithstanding, it has not been possible for contemporary Engaged Buddhists to fully embrace socialism due to the legacy of communism in Asia in the second half of the twentieth century. Not only has communism caused an immense amount of destruction of life and suffering in Asia, it has also been violently and catastrophically anti-Buddhist. In the People's Republic of China and in Cambodia, Buddhism was directly targeted and all but wiped out by the communist Maoists and the Khmer Rouge. In Vietnam, with the victory of the North Vietnamese communists, and in communist Laos, Buddhism has been constrained by varying degrees of state control. This has left communism in particular, but even socialism if not carefully qualified, as a problematic ideology for Buddhists. Again, Buddhadasa Bhikkhu has put it well:

> We can see that there are many kinds of socialism. For example, the socialism of Karl Marx is just the revenge of the worker. There's nothing to it other than revenge by the workers or laborers. Such socialism of revenge is angry and acts through its anger.[10]

Of course, Gudō lived and died well before communism unleashed its violence in Asia and thus he did not have the Engaged Buddhists' cause for drawing back from socialism. However, it must be admitted that Gudō himself voiced anger in his own writings. When he writes the following, his anger is unmistakable:

> There is a song saying, *Why are you so poor? If you want to know the reason I will tell you / That's because there are vermin that suck people's blood; / they are the emperor, the rich, and the big landowners.*

In the following passage he actually promotes anger:

[Y]ou should not forget that, for you folks, today's emperor and ministers, and in the past the Tokugawa and the daimyos from the ancient time of your ancestors, are your great enemies, against whom you should have piled up many grudges.

Gudō also occasionally directly advocated violence, writing "I hope this message will be spread to as many people as possible, people who will not be afraid even of throwing dynamite for the cause of anarchist communism" and "the hand that holds the rosary should also always hold a bomb."

It is a defining characteristic of Engaged Buddhism that its proponents practice strict, principled nonviolence on the basis of their Buddhist values. Indeed, they have engaged in a good deal of creative and extremely courageous nonviolent action in which they experiment, often at risk of their lives, with just how far adherence to nonviolence can take them in practical political struggles within the hyperviolent contexts of twentieth–twenty-first–century war and state autocracy. There is thus a significant difference between Gudō and the Engaged Buddhists with regard to violence.

A comment by the Dalai Lama sums up a good deal of this Engaged Buddhist political perspective:

> [I]nasmuch as I have any political allegiance, I suppose I am still half Marxist. I have no argument with Capitalism as long as it is practiced in a humanitarian fashion, but my religious beliefs dispose me far more towards Socialism and Internationalism. . . . Against this, I set the fact that those countries which pursue capitalist policies within a democratic framework are much freer than those which pursue the Communist ideal. . . . Having said that I remain half Marxist; if I were actually to vote in an election it would be for one of the Environmental parties.[11]

Here we see His Holiness expressing the feeling that Buddhism and socialism naturally go together, alongside his very keen awareness of the damage caused to Buddhism, and to human freedom, by communism. So while Buddhism and socialism may be a natural fit on the theoretical level, and he still feels the pull of this ideal, in practice it is impossible for him to voice support for Marxism. On the other hand, while he recognizes that human freedom flourishes relatively well in capitalist countries, His Holiness still maintains sufficient reservations about capitalism that he avoids aligning himself with it and expresses support instead for environmental parties.

There seems to be a great deal of commonality between Gudō and the Engaged Buddhists on the subjects of human equality, the need to improve the condition of the poor, and on socialism as a natural fit with Buddhism, but they part ways not only on the subject of violence but also on the subject of anarchism. For anarchism, the state as such is the enemy. Gudō was an anarchist. What did that mean to him? Certainly he viewed the particular state in which he lived as the enemy and certainly he enthusiastically embraced the anarchist valorizing of human freedom and its rejection of all forms of "power over" the individual. However, it is striking that, as Rambelli points out, Gudō never attempted to relate his anarchism to Buddhism.

The Engaged Buddhists have almost no interest in anarchism as a political system. At the time of Gudō's political career, it was possible to see anarchism as a serious political option. However, anarchism sank almost entirely from view with the defeat of the Spanish anarchists in 1939, and it was almost inevitable that the Engaged Buddhists would have little interest in it. However, on a deeper level, Engaged Buddhists neither assert a natural ideological fit between Buddhism and anarchism, nor do they regard the state per se as the enemy (though they frequently do see a particular national regime as a serious problem and struggle against it). To the contrary, some Engaged Buddhists aspire to national governance and/or have been actively involved in attempting to construct a good state.

Ambedkar was the primary author of the constitution of India when it gained independence and served as its first Law Minister. Aung San Suu Kyi almost certainly would have served as Prime Minister of Burma if she had not been prevented from doing so by that country's military government. The Dalai Lama for many years led the government in exile of Tibet and oversaw its transition to democracy. Among the Engaged Buddhists, Ariyaratne may have demonstrated the greatest sympathy for an anarchistic society. Within the context of Sri Lanka's long and deadly civil war, he advocated a devolution of power from national elites to the people themselves. He envisioned a Sri Lanka that was a loose federation of self-governing and autonomous villages, and argued that a central government that forced all people to live according to one set of rules was tyrannical. This rather anarchistic vision was far from ever gaining widespread support, however.

It seems clear that Gudō espoused anarchism and freedom from state oppression in response to the extremely harsh state tyranny under which he lived. More positively, though, we also see in his writing that he cherishes an ideal of human freedom. When he speaks of human freedom, he uses some of the most stirring and lyrical language found anywhere in his writings:

> [T]he human race has as its progenitor a mysterious holy spirit . . . that makes us progress without pause until we reach the ultimate. . . . [U]ntil now we have been struggling against the immense power of nature. Because of that struggle, today we have agriculture, animal husbandry, and industries . . . schools, churches, and books. . . .
>
> But our spirit is not satisfied with all this and, day and night, it continues fighting against our external circumstances. How long must we keep struggling before we can stop? There is no simple answer to that. However, there is something we do know. If we look at the traces left by our ancestors, and if we observe the spirit carried by the blood coursing through our arteries, there we hear the incessant sound "freedom, freedom. . . ." What is the freedom we will achieve after this struggle? To put it simply, it is being able to act always according to one's will, without ever being obstructed or bothered by anyone.

This passage evokes, perhaps, the unlikely combination of an element of buddha-nature thought (our inborn but latent buddha-nature continuously that impels us toward its own conscious self-realization, i.e., the realization of our buddhahood, our ultimate freedom) mixed with a sizable measure of Marxist historical materialism (the view that human society inevitably evolves through a variety of social forms until we reach the stage of freedom from all class oppression). That is, at the beginning of Gudō's passage, the human race has as its progenitor a "mysterious holy spirit" that impels us onward until we reach "the ultimate." At the end of the passage, that ultimate is disclosed in non-Buddhist, purely political terms as the freedom to act as one wills. Here we see how passionate Gudō is about freedom as the ultimate destiny of humankind.

The ideal of human freedom is also espoused by the Engaged Buddhists. They frequently embrace the ideal of human political freedom in the context of their advocacy of democracy and human rights, but on a deeper level, a number of Engaged Buddhists understand freedom as simultaneously essential to Buddhism, essential to what it means to be human, and essential to society. Thus, the Dalai Lama says:

> Human beings, indeed all sentient beings, have the right to pursue happiness and live in peace and in freedom. As free human beings we can use our unique intelligence to try to understand ourselves and our world. But if we are prevented from using our creative potential, we are deprived of one of the basic characteristics of a human being. It is very often the most gifted,

dedicated and creative members of our society who become victims of human rights abuses. . . . Therefore, the protection of these rights and freedoms are of immense importance both for the individuals affected and for the development of the society as a whole.[12]

Thai scholar and human rights activist Saneh Chamarik writes, "There is no need at all to search for a place of human rights in the Buddhist tradition. Freedom is indeed the essence of Buddhism."[13] Thai monk Phra Payutto elaborates on this point, giving a very "Buddhistic" defense of freedom and spiritual self-development—two values that, for him, are strongly interrelated:

[M]an is the best of trainable or educable beings. He has the potentiality of self-perfection by which a life of freedom and happiness can be realized. In order to attain this perfection, man has to develop himself physically, morally, psycho-spiritually and intellectually. . . . [T]he law of the Dharma . . . entails that every individual should be left free . . . to develop himself so that his potentiality can unfold itself and work its way towards perfection. . . . This is to say . . . that every individual has the right to self-development. . . . [The Buddha] teaches the goal of freedom that is to be reached by means of freedom and a happy means that leads to a happy end.[14]

For Payutto, freedom is both the goal and the means to the goal. His primary notion of freedom is the spiritual ideal of human perfection or buddhahood, a state of spiritual freedom. He goes on to argue that the opportunity to actualize this ideal is a fundamental human right upon which no individual, group, or state may encroach. Thus a society of ample sociopolitical freedom is necessitated by the essential nature of human being.

In conclusion, there is a great commonality of spirit between Uchiyama Gudō and the Engaged Buddhists. What Rambelli said of Gudō in his Introduction is true of the Engaged Buddhists as well: Gudō, and Engaged Buddhists, are all "not only, quite literally, free thinkers; they [are] also engaged intellectuals"; they all are attracted to "ideologies of freedom, social equality, and happiness"; and they all are experimenting with "the possibility of a progressive political agenda explicitly based on classical Buddhist thought." Gudō was ahead of his time; even today the Engaged Buddhists remain pioneers and experimenters in this territory.

Above all, what one sees when contemplating Gudō and the Engaged Buddhists is the presence of the courage and love to suffer and sometimes die for the sake of those whom their compassion compels them to help.

Part One

Chapter 1

Uchiyama Gudō:
Life and Works

Uchiyama Gudō was born on May 17, 1874 in Ojiya, Niigata Prefecture. His name before receiving Buddhist ordination was Keikichi. His father Naokichi, an impoverished artisan, had trained as both a shrine carpenter (*miya daiku*) and a wood artisan. Almost nothing is known of Gudō's life between his elementary school years and his later affiliation with the Sōtō Zen school. Yoshida Kyūichi writes that Gudō served as an in-house tutor in the household of Inoue Enryō (1858–1919), the influential Buddhist philosopher and founder of what is now Tōyō University in Tokyo, but there are no records in Inoue's archive to confirm this.[1] Inoue's family was from a town near Ojiya and he visited often, so the two men might have had some acquaintances in common with Gudō's family. It is unlikely, however, that a sophisticated intellectual such as Inoue would have employed a semiliterate country boy as private tutor for his own children.[2]

Between the time he left his village when about twenty years old and his ordination as a Zen monk in 1897, Gudō seems to have traveled in central Japan. The path to monkhood was opened to him by a relative from his mother's side, the Sōtō monk Aoyanagi Kendō. After receiving a middle-school education and religious training at various temples in Kanagawa prefecture, Gudō became the resident priest of Rinsenji in 1904, a small mountain temple in Ōhiradai near Hakone. At the time, the temple had only some forty families of parishioners (*danka*). Many were small farmers, but the land, mostly on mountainous slopes, was of poor quality and yielded little. Farmers often supplemented their modest farming income by making lacquered bowls and cups (*Hakone zaiku*) as artisans. Among the villagers, only the major landowner, Watanabe Kan'emon, was relatively wealthy.[3] In such conditions, Gudō's income as resident priest was minimal and insufficient to make a living. He grew his own vegetables and often cooked his own meals, living close to the subsistence level as did his fellow villagers.[4]

3

Gudō became interested in the rising socialist movement around 1903, and began to read the most influential socialist publication in Japan, the *Heimin shinbun*, founded that year by Kōtoku Shūsui (Kōtoku Denjirō, 1871–1911), the most charismatic figure of the early Japanese socialist movement, and others. It appears that Gudō became a socialist after reading Yano Fumio's book *Shinshakai* in 1904.[5] He met with Kōtoku and other radical intellectuals in 1905 and began to participate in their activities. Around that time, the Japanese government began to implement stricter measures to control and repress democratic organizations, a move that resulted in radicalizing the socialist and anarchist movements. This radicalization was represented by a shift from the pursuit of democratic politics through participation in elections and respect for imperial law to so-called "direct action." Based on popular mobilization (strikes, desertion, mass rallies, etc.), direct action in principle rejected representative forms of political participation and at times acknowledged recourse to extreme methods, such as terrorism (*ansatsushugi*) aimed at leading figures of the state apparatus, beginning with the emperor.[6] (It should be emphasized, however, that from the final years of the Tokugawa era until the end of World War II, terrorism in Japan was mostly connected with what we would today call "right-wing" or reactionary factions and political activities.)

Kōtoku Shūsui became an anarchist during his travels to the West Coast of the United States in 1905–1906, where he was exposed to the ideas propounded by, among others, the Russian prince Piotr Kropotkin. After his return to Japan in 1906, Kōtoku proclaimed his ideological shift, claiming that it was in accord with current trends in Europe and America, where the socialist movement was moving away from parliamentary politics toward direct revolutionary action, as embodied by the anarchist movement.[7] Under Kōtoku's leadership, the anarchists became an important component of the Japanese Socialist Party in the congress held in 1907.[8]

Gudō seems to have expressed reservations about violent direct action, but nevertheless decided to side with Kōtoku and other exponents of the direct action faction in 1907.[9] But the real trigger for Gudō's full embrace of radical anarchism was the so-called Red Flag Incident (*Akahata jiken*) of 1908. This incident began when anarchist activists left a meeting of the Socialist Party in Kanda, Tokyo, and ran in the street waving three red banners that read "Anarchism (*museifu*)," "Anarchist Communism (*museifu kyōsan*)," and "Revolution (*kakumei*)." The activists were promptly arrested by the police and imprisoned for sedition. This incident made Gudō painfully aware of the extreme state repression to which the liberation movement was subjected, a condition that asked for an equally extreme form of direct action.

Indeed, Gudō became an anarchist after the Red Flag Incident,[10] and in 1908 started a clandestine press in the back of the main hall of his temple, just behind the main altar. One of the pamphlets he authored and published, *Museifu kyōsan kakumei*, seems to have inspired another radical anarchist, Miyashita Takichi (1875–1911), to plot the assassination of the emperor. This became the pretext for the High Treason Incident (*taigyaku jiken*). Miyashita was arrested, and through him, other leading anarchists, including Kōtoku and Gudō, were also arrested and accused of high treason. According to the law at the time, "high treason" not only included actually causing harm to the emperor and his family, but also any attempt to do so, extending even to the intention of harming them. The inflammatory content of Gudō's publications, and the fact that dynamite was found at his temple, was taken as evidence of the intention to attack the emperor, and seems to have been at the basis for his conviction.[11]

After what is now considered a rigged trial, mostly based on circumstantial evidence and orchestrated by the Japanese government to get rid of the radical left, several activists were sentenced to death. Among the twenty-four people who initially received a death sentence, there were three other Buddhists in addition to Gudō: Takagi Kenmyō, Sasaki Dōgen and Mineo Setsudō. These three men had the death penalty commuted to life sentences and all later died in prison (Takagi committed suicide). Of the convicted Buddhist priests, only Gudō was executed; he was hanged on January 24, 1911. According to the trial records, the prison chaplain, a Buddhist priest, visited him just he was taken to the scaffold, but Gudō declined to talk to him and refused the rosary (*ojuzu*) that the chaplain offered him, saying, "I have no use for it. It will not make me stand in mid-air on the scaffold."[12]

After his arrest and conviction in 1909, Gudō had been asked by the Sōtō sect to resign his position as resident priest, and upon his death sentence in 1911, he was expelled from the sect.[13] Not until 1993 did the Sōtō sect restore Gudō's status as a priest and acknowledge as a mistake its own passive position toward the state's repressive policies in the early twentieth century.[14]

It is not easy to trace the development of Gudō's socialist/anarchist thought because the information we have is fragmentary. Much was based on his own life experiences of direct contact with poverty, exploitation, and ignorance; much was also due to discussions with friends and acquaintances. In this respect, the magazine *Heimin shinbun* and Kōtoku's works were certainly very influential, followed by works by fellow socialists/anarchists, and by other anarchist publications, especially the two pamphlets that Gudō published in his clandestine press. We also know that Gudō's readings included *Shinshakai* by Yano Fumio (1902),[15] "English books,"[16] and books on Western and Japanese history.[17] Concerning the latter, he read Kume Kunitake's *Nihon kodaishi*, a work that was the basis of Gudō's doubts about the sanctity of the emperor.[18] Miyashita had read a book on anarchism, *Kinsei museifushugi* (1902) by Kemuyama Sentarō (1877–1954), and it is possible that Gudō might have been exposed to some of its ideas as well.[19]

While in prison, if not before, Gudō read the Bible,[20] especially the New Testament material about Jesus. He did not believe in miracles but was attracted by the claims that Jesus would be the savior of the world.[21] However, Gudō was not interested in religious soteriology but rather in actual revolutionary thought and practice. He later expressed his admiration for Jesus's wish to spread his teachings until death,[22] and we find an echo of this admiration in his final writings from prison.

Works by Uchiyama Gudō

Gudō did not write much. In addition to about forty personal letters to family, friends, and fellow radicals,[23] and a few contributions to the *Heimin shinbun*, he published at his clandestine press Japanese translations of two anarchist pamphlets, the *Teikoku gunjin zayū no mei* and the *Museifushugi dōtoku hininron*, and authored a work on labor exploitation, state authoritarianism, and liberation politics, *Museifu kyōsan kakumei*. In addition, there remain two incomplete manuscripts, *Heibon no jikaku* and the so-called *Gokuchū shuki*, dating to the last months of his life (most likely written in prison).

Teikoku gunjin zayū no mei ("Vademecum for the Soldiers in the Imperial Army"), is a translation by Ōsugi Sakae (1885–1923) of the article *"Aux conscrits,"* originally published in the French magazine *L'anarchie* (September 27, 1906, p. 4).[24] The article is not signed, but Ōsawa Masamichi attributes it to Gustave Hervé (1871–1944),[25] a French political activist, who was first a libertarian socialist and then became a fascist. This is an antimilitarist pamphlet. The army is envisioned as the violent arm of the state, and the text emphasizes the deleterious role of the army, charging that it causes the loss of critical thinking and sensibility, xenophobia, class submission, and subjugation. The conscripts, who are most

deeply affected by this process, are thus conditioned to serve the interests of the ruling elites, described as rich bankers, speculators, and profiteers. In order to break the state's subjugation of the working masses,
the pamphlet urges conscripts to desert the military as a primary step toward carrying out the anarchist communist revolution.

The translation published by Gudō essentially follows the French
original, with some Japanese adaptations. For example, references to
France are replaced with Japan, and certain elements are eliminated
while others are simplified or explained for the benefit of Japanese readers. In general, however, the Japanese translation has a stronger, more ex-
hortative tone than the French original. The text concludes with the
"Song of Conscripts" by Christian socialist author and activist Kinoshita
Naoe (1869–1937).[26]

Museifushugi dōtoku hininron ("Anarchism and the Repudiation of
Morals"),[27] is a translation by Ōishi Seinosuke (1867–1911) of the article
"Anti-Moral Reflections" by Max Baginski (1864–1943), originally published in *Mother Earth* (vol. 2, no. 6, [August 1907]: 246–249). Baginski was
a German-born American anarchist active in New York, editor of the
magazine *Freedom*, and an early collaborator with the political activist
Emma Goldman (1869–1940), especially in her magazine, *Mother Earth.*

The pamphlet published by Gudō includes a few lines not found in
Baginski's original text, which can be attributed to Gudō himself; he also
included passages from Pierre-Joseph Proudhon.[28] These few sentences
emphasize the anarchist refusal of the state and its institutions, the rejection of private property. They also contain a critique of the content of
public education, the claim that anarchism is a revolt of individuals to
protect themselves from harassment from the state and related organizations, and a scathing critique of ethics and religion as lackeys of the
predatory machine of the state.

This pamphlet contains a strong indictment of bourgeois morality as
it was taught at the time—an ethics of decorum, restraint, absolute respect for private property, and unquestioning submission to the law.
Baginski argues that this morality was invented by the ruling elites in
order to replace the waning power of religion and by the monarchy to
control the subaltern masses. By thus replacing the source of moral judgment, Baginski notes, the basis for subjugation also shifts from the outside (social institutions, coercion) to the inside (the interiority) of the individual: what is variously called inner voice, moral conscience, duty,
etc. Baginski also offers evidence of the fundamental hypocrisy of this
moral system, which prevents the proletariat from improving its

wretched condition while ignoring the exploitation, profiteering, and war mongering of the ruling classes.

The pamphlet also addresses sex, which, in certain areas of the anarchist galaxy, was held to be an unconstrained activity between free and consentient individuals (what came to be called "free sex"), rather than an activity that could be subject to the control and coercion of social and religious norms and conventions.

The Japanese translation follows the English original, with some elisions and occasional additional explanations. Priests in the original text become Buddhist monks (*sōryo*) in the Japanese translation, while rulers become emperors (*teiō*). The additional lines added by Gudō at the beginning and end are a concise introduction to his own vision of anarchism.

Museifu kyōsan kakumei (Nyūgoku kinen) ("Anarchist Communist Revolution: In Commemoration of Imprisonment"), Gudō's first extensive work, was written after the Red Flag Incident (*Akahata jiken*) of June 1908, in which anarchist activists took to the street in Tokyo, waving banners advocating "Anarchy" (*museifu*), "Anarchist Communism" (*museifu kyōsan*), and "Revolution" (*kakumei*). Gudō chose these three words as the title of his text. He printed between 1,000 and 2,000 copies of the pamphlet in his clandestine press, and mailed them in packets of fifty to former subscribers of *Heimin shinbun*. This text seems to have aroused very strong emotions in its readers; some recipients were so afraid of its revolutionary content that they burned the pamphlet, while others brought it to the police to avoid charges of co-responsibility in its dissemination. As previously noted, Miyashita claimed that its content inspired him to plan and attempt to carry out a plot to kill the emperor.

High treason trial records define this pamphlet as the "the most evil writing in the entire Japanese history," especially because Gudō harshly criticized the contemporary imperial system and denied, in very derogatory terms, the divine nature of the emperor.[29] As the subtitle "Why is life so hard for tenant farmers?" suggests, Gudō conceived this text as a sermon directed to tenant farmers (perhaps his own parishioners). Accordingly, it is written in a simple language and presents simple ideas, though in an incendiary style.

Heibon no jikaku ("Common Consciousness" or "Becoming Aware of the Obvious") presents a more systematic treatment of Gudō's religious and political ideals. This is an incomplete manuscript that was returned to Gudō's relatives after his execution,[30] and it is not clear when he actually wrote it. Morinaga suggests that it was written at Rinsenji before the incarceration, and "certainly before the Red Flag Incident of June 22,

1908."[31] However, Yoshida defines this work as a manifestation of "democratic idealism" and the "final point of Gudō's thought."[32] Its content is more developed and systematic than what we find in *Museifu kyōsan kakumei*, indicating that it is a later work. References to self-sacrifice and spiritual preparation for the scaffold also suggest that it was indeed written in prison, as does the fact that it is unlikely that the police would have allowed Gudō to keep this manuscript with him at the time of his arrest. Also, no explicit references are made to socialism or anarchism, perhaps in order to avoid police censorship.

The title is somewhat ironic. It refers, literally, to the a "common (if not commonplace) consciousness," which is both the political awareness of the proletariat (the commoners) and an awareness of obvious things, as it were. This is a form of revolutionary consciousness that all individuals should develop in order to carry out a revolutionary transformation of society, what Gudō defines, uncannily, as the "realization of paradise" on Earth. As the basis of revolutionary awareness and action, this is indeed a collection of "obvious truths"; on the other hand, the fact that these truths require considerable effort to be understood and digested makes them not quite so obvious. At the same time, the text also describes the commoners' process of attaining awareness of the social mechanisms that generate their subjugation and, once understood and denied, their liberation.

In the text, Gudō sets out to define the necessary state of mind (consciousness) that would lead individuals and communities to the realization of an ideal anarchic society. Gudō originally planned to write about six increasingly larger dimensions of such a consciousness, from the individual, the family, and the workplace (the factory and agriculture), to the municipality, the state, and the entire world. Rather than serving as a blueprint for action, this document combines ontology and political economy infused with significant religious themes. The manuscript, however, ends before treating the subjects of national and world consciousness.[33]

Gokuchū shuki ("Prison Manuscript") is a fragment containing Gudō's highly personal reflections on his own moral principles and the reasons for his political engagement. It begins with emphasizing the need to adhere to one's individual principles and act accordingly. He also argues that each person's principles all have something in common: the desire for just working conditions and fair living standards for all. Most of the text contains a critique of the huge gap separating rich from poor and the wretched condition of the workers, and it suggests that the elimination of wealth disparity would result in more resources becoming equally available to all. It appeals to moderation: "we don't want . . . luxuries," he writes, "we only ask for" a ten-hour workday, one day off every week, a chance to buy clothes appropriate to the seasons, health care, a certain amount of leisure, and the possibility to pursue personal religious beliefs.

The fragment ends with Gudō's meditations on the sense of self-realization, even joy, that derive from the consciousness of having lived and acted according to one's just principles. After mentioning Śākyamuni, the Greek philosopher Diogenes, and Jesus Christ, as well as famous Edo-period champions of social virtue such as Sakura Sōgorō and Ōshio Heihachirō, Gudō writes that he is ready to give up his life, either on the scaffold or in a maximum-security prison in cold Hokkaidō. Ominously, however, the text ends before Gudō spells out the "method" (hōhō) whereby one might achieve imperturbability in the face of personal disaster, and without defining a clear and intimate sense of "happiness in life" (jinsei no kōfuku).

Chapter 2

A Buddhist Anarchism

In this chapter I explore the major intellectual components of Gudō's attempts to bridge his own understanding of Buddhism with contemporary developments within international socialism (in particular, the emergence of anarchism as a major component of the workers' revolutionary movement). He also sought to connect this understanding with images of Christianity, and a more or less direct influence from other traditional forms of Japanese thought and social activism.

By the end of the Tokugawa period, Japan had embarked on a systematic process of modernization that opened up its participation in the global capitalist economy. Among other developments of this modernization there were deep and extensive social transformations, including the formation of a working class. The contradictions generated by the newly imported systems and the attendant social problems that afflicted workers—not only the proletariat, but farmers, artisans, and impoverished intellectuals as well—were also discussed by other Buddhist activists, most notably Sada Kaiseki (1818–1882).[1]

In a parallel development, since the end of the nineteenth century, we encounter a diffusion of socialist thought in a wide spectrum of positions, ranging from moderate democratic socialism and Christian visions of society to radical anarchist communism. The impact of Marx and Engels began to be felt only relatively late in Japan.[2] At first, Japanese activists adopted ideas and representations from Christian socialism, Russian populism, and various democratic and libertarian movements from the Anglo-Saxon world.[3] It is from within this complex social and cultural arena, one of powerful social changes and equally powerful ideas of social renewal and revolution, that Uchiyama Gudō's works and activities must be situated.

Golden Words

In 1903 the socialist newspaper *Heimin shinbun* published a call for readers' contributions on the theme "Why I became a socialist." Gudō sent in his personal considerations, which were published early in the following year.

> Mr. Uchiyama Gudō (Hakone, Sagami Prefecture): As a Buddhist preacher (*dendōsha*), these are the golden words that constitute the basis of my religious faith, namely, "All sentient beings have buddha-nature," "This Dharma is undifferentiated and there is no high and low in it," and "All sentient beings are my children." When I discovered that what socialism says is in perfect accord with these maxims, I became a believer (*shinja*) in socialism.[4]

Gudō obviously understood Buddhism as a religion that taught equality and the need to care for the oppressed and the dispossessed. Let us take a closer look at the scriptural passages he quoted.

First, "All sentient beings have buddha-nature" is a well-known sentence from the *Great Nirvana Sutra*,[5] and has been long used in Japan and elsewhere to justify the universal possibility for salvation typical of Mahayana Buddhism. It is worth noting, however, that the universal possibility of salvation—envisioned as "becoming a buddha" (*jōbutsu*) either in a present or future lifetime—does not normally imply social equality. In fact, Japanese Buddhism historically contributed to the formation of ideas and practices of social differentiation and discrimination, based at least in part on Indian theories of castes. These are most evident in the development of separate funeral rituals and the attribution of posthumous Buddhist names according to age, gender, profession, and social standing.[6]

The next passage indicated by Gudō, "This Dharma is undifferentiated and there is no high and low in it," is from the *Diamond Sutra*.[7] As the context makes clear, this sentence, in line with the general argument of the entire scripture, refers to issues pertaining to epistemology and ontology, rather than to social structure. Accordingly, the undifferentiated nature (Skt. *samatā*, Jp. *byōdō*) of the Buddhist Dharma refers to emptiness (Skt. *śūnyatā*, Jp. *kū*), not to social equality.

Finally, the third scriptural passage, "All sentient beings are my children," is from the *Lotus Sutra*.[8] The complete passage reads:

> All sentient beings are my children, but they are deeply attached to worldly pleasures and lack wisdom. There is no peace in the three worlds like in a house on fire; they are full of sufferings and have to be greatly feared.[9]

This sentence has been interpreted as meaning that the Buddha employs expedient means (Skt. *upāya*, Jp. *hōben*) in order to save sentient beings from their wretched condition of ignorance and attachment: the "house on fire." What is interesting is that the *Lotus Sutra* explicitly refers to attachment to "worldly pleasures"—something that certainly does not apply to the dispossessed peasants who constituted the vast majority of Gudō's temple parishioners. A common theme might be lack of wisdom, understood by Gudō as the consciousness of the social conditions that cause poverty and subjugation. Following the *Lotus Sutra*, Gudō believed that his duty as a Buddhist priest was to save beings from suffering.

Gudō's choice of passages from Buddhist scriptures is interesting, but unfortunately we do not know the interpretive processes that led him to his selection. It seems that Gudō chose those passages out of context and re-signified them in a socialist fashion by translating Buddhist soteriology (salvation) as social liberation, the epistemology of emptiness (*kū*) and undifferentiation (*byōdō*) as bases for egalitarian politics, and the doctrine of expedient means as a blueprint for social and political activism. Had he developed these theoretical issues further, he might have been able to provide Japanese Buddhists with a powerful Buddhist "theology of liberation." But Gudō was no theoretician; as we shall see, rather than devoting his time to writing about revolutionary theory he was more deeply concerned with the condition of the dispossessed peasants and, to a lesser extent, of the industrial proletariat, and he thought that it was his mission to try to improve their lives.[10]

Despite Gudō's explicit reference to Buddhist sources for his socialist beliefs, however, we should also note that his longer writings, in particular *Museifu kyōsan kakumei* and *Heibon no jikaku*, contain very few indisputably Buddhist elements. In fact, when in *Museifu kyōsan kakumei* Gudō describes the hardships faced by tenant farmers, he explicitly rejects Buddhist notions of one's suffering in the present life as the result of past karma and instead attributes their hardships to "superstitions." By superstitions he meant the supposed need to uphold the existing social order based on hierarchy and exploitation, to which tenant farmers were subjected both by their landowners (to whom they pay land rents) and the state (to which they pay taxes and send off their sons as soldiers). However, the underlying rhetoric of "awaken[ing] . . . from . . . long superstitious dreams" echoes Zen Buddhist soteriology of personal engagement and responsibility. The idea of awakening, especially in its social and revolutionary form as awareness or consciousness (*jikaku*), is the subject of Gudō's incomplete manuscript entitled *Heibon no jikaku*.

Selfless Love

Another important thread in Gudō's intellectual and political development is the Buddhist movement known as *Muga no ai* ("Selfless Love"). Jōdo Shinshū priest and scholar Itō Shōshin (1876–1963), invoking the need for a spiritual revolution, established the organization Mugaen ("Garden of Selflessness") and began to publish the magazine *Muga no ai* ("Selfless Love") in 1905. Itō envisioned "selfless love," in itself a development of the classical Buddhist idea of compassion (Skt. *karuṇa,* Jp. *jihi*), as the supreme truth (*zettai no shinri*) and the ultimate essence of the entire universe (*uchū no shinsō*). He wrote:

> [E]ach individual being that constitutes the universe is, in its true essence (*shinsō*) the result of the activity of selfless love. The activity of selfless love refers to the fact that each individual being completely entrusts one's individual destiny to the others, but at the same time loves the others with all of its energies.[11]

Several socialists, including Kōtoku Shūsui, Sakai Toshihiko, in addition to Gudō, showed interest in the Muga no ai movement. Gudō wrote letters of appreciation to the magazine and claimed deep spiritual and intellectual affinities with the project. The ideas of Muga no ai were not very distant from ideas of mutual aid put forth between the second half of the nineteenth and the early twentieth centuries by various socialist and anarchist thinkers such as Pierre-Joseph Proudhon (1809–1865) and Piotr Kropotkin (1842–1921), which were also a reaction against contemporary social Darwinism that emphasized force, coercion, and selfishness. Mutual aid was indeed one of the main tenets of Gudō's political thought.[12] He explicitly criticized the idea that "human beings are just a kind of animal" and that their "animal nature . . . forces them to ignore others in order to satisfy their own desires." Instead, he wrote:

> The family, the state, the entire world, they are all aggregations of individuals, and if each individual simply lived and acted according to pure-hearted kindness—that is, with a spirit of independence and freedom, the will to help the weak, and caring for one's neighbor—we would all be able to lead a peaceful and perfect collective life.[13]

Later in 1905, when Itō publicly abandoned the Jōdo Shinshū denomination as an attempt to shake the religious establishment—a move that had a wide resonance at the time—Gudō was deeply impressed. However, he decided to continue serving as a resident priest in his village.

He explained his thinking in a letter to Itō that was published in *Muga no ai* (no. 13, December 10, 1905):

> [T]he people in the place where I, thanks to fortunate chance, am now a resident priest, have been under the beliefs of the Sōtō sect for 300 years, but the poor fellows not only do not know the personality of our patriarch Dōgen, they don't even know his name. If I abandoned them, it would be impossible to plant Buddha seeds in this place for thousands of *kalpa*s. Thus, until my sect's administration (*honzan*) dismisses me of my duties as a resident priest, I am ready to fight with all my energy with the truth of selflessness as my sword.[14]

This letter shows Gudō's strong intention, at least at this point in his life, to continue as a resident priest in order to spread Buddhism among his fellow villagers. Earlier, he had told the socialist leader and author Ishikawa Sanshirō, "If one does not intend to spend all one's life in this place, there is no hope to save the people here."[15] In his view, preaching Buddhism was identical to spreading socialist ideas, as both aimed to improve the living conditions of the people. Indeed, Gudō was not only a socialist activist but also a serious practitioner of Zen. His 1910 arrest occurred upon his return from a retreat period at Eiheiji, the monastic center of Sōtō Zen. His letter in *Muga no ai* concludes with the following words:

> My friends, in my temple there is no Muga no ai sign, but it is certainly such a place, so please do not hesitate to visit me for both self-cultivation and preaching activities. Even though mine is a bare residence where I live a modest life as a celibate, for us who abide in selfless love, I will make it a comfortable place to advance day by day toward enlightenment with the company of the vast and long tongue of nature.[16]

Engaged Buddhism

Initially, Gudō was looking for ways to spread socialism within a Buddhist framework. In a letter to the *Heimin shinbun* (January 1904), he wrote:

> In my opinion, if the socialist ideals were preached today by the aristocracy and the millionaires after acquiring [revolutionary] consciousness so as to abandon their properties and their positions and become just ordinary persons, like our master Prince Siddhārtha did, [it would be easier to convince the rest of the people. But] if they do not do so, it will be difficult to put in practice the gospel. If you agree even just a little with these foolish ideas of mine, I would greatly appreciate if someone could teach me methods to convince aristocrats and millionaires.[17]

As we can see, Prince Siddhārtha was a model for social action as well as of religious activity for Gudō. Morinaga Eizaburō suggests that Gudō had the wealthy villager Watanabe Kan'emon in mind when he wrote this letter. If he could convince Kan'emon, the wealthiest man and biggest landowner in Ōhiradai, to become a socialist and renounce his property, Gudō reasoned that all the other villagers would easily follow his example and thus an anarchist community would be created.[18] But whether or not Gudō had an actual person in mind, the gist of this letter—first convert the wealthy and the powerful to socialism, then all the other citizens will follow their example—resonates with similar ideas in his other writings: "[W]e should first urge the persons of influence to build many public facilities and let villagers enjoy them,"[19] and

> The capitalist who has acquired consciousness will reject the old crime of living out of his capital and will come to realize that all human beings must secure their clothing and food through their own labor. . . . After making his own capital available to all without compensation as a common resource for livelihood, he will think of how best to employ his talent and labor in order to realize as soon as possible such (i.e., anarchist) paradise.[20]

Gudō's idea of a political transformation by example, in which people follow enlightened upper-class leaders, reminds us not of Leninism, in which the proletariat serves as the vanguard that is given the responsibility of leading the other workers, but more of anarchists such as Piotr Kropotkin, a member of the top echelons of the Russian aristocracy who became a leading and influential anarchist thinker.[21]

In the Japanese context, we find analogous Confucian values, especially as they were reinterpreted in the Edo-period tradition of popular revolt (again, the cases of Sakura Sōgorō and Ōshio Heihachirō are emblematic in this respect), as well as the Buddhist doctrine of the universal king (*cakravartin*), who conquers and rules in a peaceful way by means of his own virtue.[22] More directly related to Gudō, the book *Shinshakai* by Yano Fumio, which awakened Gudō's interest in socialism, described his "new society" as a monarchy enlightened by the wisdom of the emperor, the intelligence of scholars, and the altruism of the capitalists.[23] Kōtoku Shūsui also argued that socialism could be realized under ethical (and, we should add, mythological) rulers such as the Chinese King Wen and the Japanese Emperor Nintoku.[24]

It is also noteworthy that the first socialist political organization in Japan, the Tōyō shakaitō (Oriental Socialist Party, formed and immediately outlawed and disbanded in 1882), heralded as a model of socialism the acts of the feudal lord Nabeshima, who, in a time of general penury, allowed destitute peasants to use the lands of the wealthy.[25]

Gudō's tenure as resident priest at Rinsenji was not the first time he had directly experienced the dire conditions of the dispossessed. During his elementary school years in the 1880s, the Japanese government was implementing deflationary policies that resulted in widespread impoverishment in the countryside. In Gudō's area, people experienced famine and devastating poverty, further aggravated by the government's imposition that they continue to pay taxes.[26] Ojiya was also the home of some two dozen wealthy landowners, among whom the Nishiwaki family, the most prominent, employed about 800 sharecroppers.[27]

Morinaga Eizaburō has argued that the disastrous effects of state policies on the proletariat and the exploitation of the sharecroppers by big landowners, witnessed by Gudō as a youth, were the basis for his powerful descriptions in *Museifu kyōsan kakumei* pamphlet and the prison fragment.[28] Gudō was seriously concerned about the living conditions of his parishioners and strove to provide them with means to overcome their condition. In an article written for the *Heimin shinbun* in 1904, socialist activist Ishikawa Sanshirō reports the following words by Gudō:

> Since old times, the main occupation of the people in this area has been woodwork. However, people here are indeed narrow-minded and deeply traditionalist (*korō*), and are unable to attempt any grand enterprise. In particular, individualist egoism is strong, and common endeavors are very hard to organize. Their land income would be enough to succeed, to an extent, in forestry-related activities, but they simply cross their hands. Concerning industry and other productive activities, even though their skills are somewhat developed, they cannot gain much income from that. As a consequence, poverty greatly increases day by day, month by month; the residents themselves are conscious that in a few years they will end up losing their houses and their jobs and will no longer be able to live here, but no one has the will to try to save them from this situation. Each of them just hungers for small individual profit and competes with all the others, therefore helping the capitalists make even larger profits. This is really lamentable. I have realized that I should not talk with the adults, so I put all my efforts in teaching only children and adolescents.[29]

Gudō's revolutionary platform is expounded in *Museifu kyōsan kakumei*. The text makes a number of important arguments, which can be summarized in the following eight points:

1. The land is a natural resource and as such should not belong to any individual, but instead should be commonly owned and cultivated.

2. Each individual should live off his/her own work; one's work should be based on one's tastes and capacities, and one's surplus should be used to balance other people's deficiencies.

3. Accumulation of private capital should be avoided, and all wealth should be shared (in fact, tenant farmers are urged to ransack the landowners' storehouses and "take back" what the landowners have accumulated through their "theft" of the tenants' labor).

4. The state government is an instrument of oppression of the workers and should be eliminated; taxation and military conscription are especially odious.

5. The head of the government, the emperor, is not divinely descended, as state propaganda maintains, but rather a descendant of "murderers and thieves" from a "remote corner of Kyushu." Gudō likens him to infamous figures (brigands and monsters) in Japanese folklore, such as Nagasunebiko, Kumasaka Chōhan, and Shuten Dōji.

6. War is caused by the state and not by its citizens; by abolishing the state one will bring an end to the causes for war all over the world.

7. Anarchist communism is the solution: it begins by forming labor unions and expanding their impact from the village to the state to the entire world; at that point, the ideal of anarchist communism, i.e., to ensure freedom and a comfortable life to all, will be realized.

8. To achieve his revolutionary movement requires self-sacrifice and readiness to use violence ("throwing dynamite").

Gudō did not spell out his political program for the revolutionary transformation of society in *Museifu kyōsan kakumei*, however. That comes up to some extent in *Heibon no jikaku*, where Gudō argues that the acquisition of consciousness will transform the way people see themselves, their place in society, and the way they live. The family, as the smallest and most intimate human group, is at the center of his program of revolutionary transformation. The head of the household will become the coordinator of family activities and the moderator in its members' discussions, a sort of *primus inter pares*. His primary role is to lead the other family members to awaken their own consciousness, and in order to do so, he must share food and chores with equanimity and help take care of the children from a very young age. It is particularly important that he set an egalitarian example for the other family members, especially the children (whom he must teach to act according to their own proclivities), as they represent the future free individuals of the anarchic paradise; and the elders, who are the most difficult to educate to the new social model.

Gudō also treats women as equal to men, as equally autonomous and free individuals; he emphasizes that women should also work autonomously outside of the family, both in order to contribute to the family income and to be more independent of their husbands and male relatives.

In the workplace, Gudō emphasizes the need to establish industrial trade unions and transform factories into collective property belonging to the workers. He proposes a universal economic plan in which the demand and supply for each commodity in the entire world will be assessed; production will accordingly be distributed among the various industrial centers. While this idea can be seen today as being extremely abstract and naïve, more interesting is Gudō's suggestion that "manufacturing should be carried out as close as possible to the place of production of raw materials," in line with his general emphasis on autonomous but closely interrelated communities.

Gudō is more skeptical about the development of socialist consciousness among farmers, which he believed would occur later and as a result of industrial workers' consciousness. This skepticism may be based on his own experiences with the tenant farmers at his temple. He describes agricultural workers as generally more conservative, more influenced by feudal mores, and thus devoid of the spirit of initiative. In any case, as a result of this consciousness, the land will become common property—as it used to be in the ancient past, when the ancestors worked the land as a natural space, together and without private property rights. Ultimately, all individuals will have to make a living through their own labor; living off acquired capital will no longer be possible.

In addition to the fact that capitalists and landowners should turn their property into communal assets, Gudō proposes the establishment of workers' relief funds (insurance) and free and universal education and health care. Also significant is his emphasis on workers' welfare outside of work. He proposes the creation of recreational "clubs" where members can pursue their interests, deepen their education and knowledge, and refine their artistic tastes.

Consciousness will also change communal life and the administration of municipalities. Gudō begins with the hypothesis that in the distant past, all people lived in the same condition in villages, where all resources were held in common. He describes a process of primitive accumulation in which people's misfortunes due to "natural disasters and individual predispositions" were exploited by a few individuals to accumulate capital. This was the beginning of the gap between poor and rich, a situation that will be redressed in the new anarchist society.

While the final goal is collective property, as an intermediary (and more realistic) stage, Gudō proposes the formation of collective funds in the municipalities, which would be used to establish schools and hospitals free to all residents, and free recreational facilities where residents can have friendly interactions without barriers of class, gender, or age. Particularly important is free public education for working-class children, which will give them the opportunity to develop their work skills and attitudes so that they can become active and autonomous workers.

The Quest for an
Anarchist Paradise

We can identify another important thread in Gudō's Buddhist socialism, more deeply related to the very nature of the Buddhist sangha and its traditional policies and methods of governance. During the interrogation for the High Treason Incident trial, Gudō was asked when he became a socialist. He replied that in 1904,

> when I saw, in documents previously collected by my sect, the places where Buddhist monks practice in China, in which two or three hundred people gather together, wear the same clothes, eat the same food, and live in collectivity, I thought how beautiful it was. I came to embrace the ideal that, if such a system were to be implemented in one village, in one district, in one country, this would be a very good system. At the time, I happened to read the *Heimin shinbun,* and I realized that it was about the same ideology that I embraced. At that point I became a socialist of the anarchist communist kind.[30]

It is interesting that Gudō explicitly connected the social ideals of socialism, and in particular of anarchist communism, with the collective, monastic life of the Buddhist sangha in its non-reformed, traditional ways, as was still the case in China at the time.[31]

It has been argued that traditional Buddhism developed two different interpretations of Dharma: one refers to secular, personal morality (closer to the Hindu concept of *svadharma*); the other is an absolute, uncompromising respect for the basic moral tenets of Buddhism as simplified in the ten virtues. While the former concept of Dharma applies primarily to kingship, with its need to compromise on moral considerations (the use of violence, social hierarchy, etc.) and the related possibility of a negative karmic retribution, the latter is the arena of Buddhist renunciant ascetics. An example of the former is Emperor Aśoka; Prince Vessantara, with his absolute and unwavering allegiance to his vow of generosity, is a typical example of the latter.[32] It would at first appear that Gudō followed more closely the second interpretation of Dharma, as an absolute paradigm of morality; however, he applies it not only to Buddhist ascetics but to all individuals as a way to establish a utopian society.

Utopian visions are not unknown throughout the long history of Buddhism. Ideal models of kingship such as the *cakravartin* (universal moral ruler), or eschatological visions based on the advent of Maitreya, the future Buddha, are typical examples of such utopias. What is interesting is that Buddhist utopias tend to envision an egalitarian and non-violent society, in which people live out of natural resources through their own labor, as presented in the *Aggañña Sutta*.[33] In fact, the establishment of kingship, according to that scripture, is envisioned as a way to end the social conflicts that arise from the development of social differentiations and private property. In this view, kingship is not the ideal political form but merely a lesser evil related to the impossibility of preserving an anarchist society.

In terms of political thought, classical Buddhism oscillates between systematic legitimization of existing forms of kingship (which, in exchange, must support Buddhist institutions and protect the autonomy of the sangha) and the organization of the Buddhist sangha as an autonomous social organization. Various authors have indicated that the constitution of the sangha is essentially democratic and republican, if not quite socialistic. It is characterized, among other things, by its prohibition against individual property, common ownership of property, communal life, and decisions based on collective deliberation.[34] In East Asia in particular, millenarian revolts were sometimes inspired by Buddhist teachings, and some radical movements had libertarian and anarchistic components.[35]

It is therefore not impossible to find a significant continuity between one thread of traditional Buddhist thought and practice, which envisions the sangha as an idealized utopia in localized and clearly self-contained social space (that of arbitrary and exploitative kingship), what Michel Foucault called a "heterotopia,"[36] and Gudō's anarchism. An important difference, though, is that Gudō tried to extend the classical ideals of the sangha (to which he indeed refers directly) to the entire society through a radical critique of contemporary Japanese kingship. In this, he was closer to premodern utopian revolutionaries than to classical Buddhist thinkers.

An Anarchist Animism?

The section on individual consciousness of *Heibon no jikaku* is particularly interesting for its originality. Gudō posits the existence of a "mysterious holy spirit" (*fukashigi no seirei*) as the "father of the human race."[37] This spirit is immortal and is passed down, through blood, from our ancestors to our descendants. Gudō seems to have understood such a spirit as both an autonomous entity and a metaphor (i.e., the spirit of freedom), and it is in this latter sense that a father should "infuse one's spirit that has acquired consciousness" into a child from the time it "wears diapers."[38] This spirit is the agency behind the human race's incessant struggle, first against nature in order to acquire freedom from need, then against social and political oppression: in "the traces left by our ancestors, and . . . [in] the spirit carried by the blood coursing through our arteries, we hear the incessant sound 'freedom, freedom.'"[39]

Our goal is to become conscious of this natural propensity for freedom inscribed in our spirit by acquiring consciousness of our present condition, our oppression, and the possibility to become free. Consciousness is related to a spiritual progress (literally, a progressive improvement of our spirit) that takes place thanks to "schools, churches, and books." Of course, we also have a bodily dimension, exemplified by Gudō in terms of necessary commodities (food, clothing, and shelter) and economic activities to provide for them; the body is the seat of material desires.

This kind of anarchist animism, as it were, is combined with a peculiar political soteriology. First of all, the new society in which Gudō's ideals are to be realized is defined as "what the old sages called paradise (*tengoku*) or [the] land of the gods (*shinkoku*)."[40] The term "paradise," in particular, occurs nine times in the manuscript, and is envisioned as a realm of peace and social equality. One wonders about the impact on Gudō's thought of late Edo-period religious movements that aimed at a radical transformation of society (*yonaoshi*); in Europe as well, socialist and anarchist movements, at least in their grass-roots forms, were deeply steeped in folk eschatology.

The second soteriological component is the striking idea of a double path awaiting human beings, one of "annihilation" (*horobi*) and the other of "eternal life" (*eisei*).[41] People who do not acquire consciousness and those who do yet choose not to act accordingly, are destined to annihilation. In contrast, those who act according to their revolutionary consciousness will achieve eternal life precisely because of their involvement, no matter how marginal, "in the realization of paradise."

We also find a hint of possible worldly rewards for the conscious person and revolutionary hero, namely, the chance to "bask in one's holy spirit" as well as being "able to engage in self-cultivation in everyday life."[42] It would seem that conscious action brings one's innate spirit to the fore; this spirit would put forth the "light of freedom" and "bestow its blessings upon all," and one of these blessings is the possibility to "engage in self-cultivation."[43] In Gudō's other writings, the term "self-cultivation" (shūyō) refers to Zen practice, but it is not clear what it actually means in the context of the *Heibon no jikaku* manuscript.

This work contains a number of references to Christianity:[44] in addition to paradise and soteriology, we find the New Testament parable of the grain of wheat; revolutionary martyrs are called "persons most loved by god"; and churches are indicated, together with schools and books, as one of the things that ensure the "continuous improvement and progress of our spirit." Unfortunately, we do not know enough of Gudō's intellectual trajectory in his final years to evaluate the role of Christianity in his thought. However, we should not ignore the fact that Gudō's soteriology does not presuppose another world, but takes place in this world as a consequence of one's involvement (or lack thereof) and self-sacrifice in the revolutionary movement. In this respect, immortality and annihilation seem to be used as metaphors for eternal memory and forgetfulness among the revolutionaries. Gudō's "god" who loves revolutionary martyrs is perhaps just an image intended to ennoble anarchist heroes in a way that would not be possible through references to Buddhism. Indeed, it is hard to imagine, in a modern Japanese context, buddhas or bodhisattvas "loving" revolutionary heroes.

Direct Action, Doubt, and Self-sacrifice

As we have already seen, Gudō came to embrace anarchism at a time when the international anarchist movement was shifting away from representative politics and engaging more and more in direct, sometimes violent, action. Gudō was also deeply shocked by the Red Flag Incident of 1908, which made him painfully aware of the power of state repression, to which the liberation movement was subject in Japan. This condition seemed to call for an equally extreme form of direct action.

Gudō's embrace of violent anarchism is described rather explicitly in a letter to Itō:

[T]here is nothing more violent than the government—any government. It employs weapons to oppress the people and steal tax money from them. The power of the priests (*shūkyōka*) is useless to restrain this violence. If priests today are really serious about creating a paradise, they must first overthrow the government. The hand that holds the rosary (*juzu*) should also always hold a bomb.[45]

This incendiary statement reveals both the sense of impotence felt by Gudō in his revolutionary effort, which, we should remember, was essentially aimed at securing a decent life for all, beginning with his temple parishioners, and his adhesion to radical, direct-action anarchism, namely, terrorism (*ansatsushugi*) targeting leading government figures from the head of state down.[46] It is important to place statements like this in historical context. At the time Gudō was writing these words, Japan was a very different country from today; in particular, the years between 1905 and 1918 were marked by numerous strikes and insurrections, partly fueled by workers' awareness that their interests were not adequately represented in official politics.

In any case, the moral legitimacy of the use of violence against a tyrannical, oppressive social system is an endlessly disputed subject. Buddhism too, despite its systematic upholding of nonviolence, developed the idea that it was legitimate to "kill one so that many may live" (*issatsu tashō*),[47] and the range and complexity of Buddhist attitudes toward warfare (which may be extended to include class struggle) indicates that Gudō was by no means alone in this position.[48]

Another event that deeply influenced Gudō at the time was a quarrel between rival factions among workers employed in the construction of a dam for an hydroelectric plant in the Hakone mountains. When the quarrel escalated, sixty workers attacked their rivals with dynamite; one person died and a few others were injured. This incident taught Gudō for the first time the power of the working classes. In a letter to Ishikawa Sanshirō dated June 8, 1907 he wrote: "[O]n this occasion I realized for the first time how great is the force of the workers," and he began to think of how to "guide this force in the most useful way toward the supreme happiness of humanity."[49]

A growing pessimism toward nonviolent action and also a sense of intellectual confusion is well expressed in another letter to Ishikawa, dated December 6, 1907:

Religion, past the age in which it was one with politics, has now been separated from it; ours is a time in which politics uses religion [for its own ends]. The person devoted to the way of the gods (*kami no michi*) cannot subject himself to a politics that only cares about its own interests, can he? I personally believe that a time will come in the near future when the people will live, each according to one's absolute faith (*zettai no shinkō*), without the need for politics, and I also believe that it is my mission to act so that this will happen as soon as possible.[50]

This is a strange and confused letter, both in its vocabulary and content. Gudō indicates a personal urge to contribute to accelerating the revolutionary process and, in the context of contemporary anarchism, that would have meant support for direct action and terrorism. However, the wording is ambiguous. Gudō calls "religion"—and, of course, also his own activity—"the way of the gods" (*kami no michi*), an expression normally referring to Shinto (which at that time was the religious-ideological basis of the Japanese imperial system). Gudō also writes of an "absolute faith" (*zettai no shinkō*), by which he probably means an uncompromised and uncompromising personal belief. Finally, he argues that his own mission, as a Buddhist anarchist, is to accelerate the advent of the age in which politics will be unnecessary and absolute faith will triumph. This sounds uncannily like the statement of a religious fundamentalist terrorist, but Gudō did not have a clear religious program to advance, aside from his own version of anarchist communism—which, as we have seen, was often characterized in religious terms.

Gudō's message is clearer if we interpret "politics" (*seiji*) as referring specifically to the state government (*seifu*). In this case, what he seems to advocate is not a vague anti-political struggle but an action against the authoritarian state, aimed at the liberation of its citizens in order to allow them to hold on to their most deeply felt beliefs. In any case, we can argue that these ambiguities (Politics in general or state government in particular? Religion or politics? Buddhism or anarchism?) made the message of the early Japanese anarchists too confusing to be taken seriously by the masses, and at the same time too extreme to be tolerated by the authorities.

This letter perhaps also indicates a deeper, personal vacillation in Gudō's revolutionary endeavor. In fact, in the records of the High Treason trial, Gudō is reported as testifying:

> At the time [before the arrest], I was a follower of anarchist communism. In short, I believed that a class struggle between the anarchist communists and the dominant classes was unavoidable, and I wanted to participate in this movement with a spirit of sacrifice, that is, even at the cost of my own life.

Therefore, it is true that I agreed with Kōtoku's theory of violent revolution, but I did think that it was still too soon for that. I mean, in such a time of police interference it was impossible to carry out spoken and written propaganda in the open; rather, I believed that it was strategically preferable for the unfolding of our mission to make propaganda through secret publications and gather many comrades in that way.[51]

Statements like this seem to indicate that Gudō deemed propaganda more effective than violence, but that he had decided to follow his friends. In particular, he overcame his initial reluctance toward violent action when he knew that Kōtoku's medical condition had worsened and he did not have much longer to live. It thus became imperative to start the revolution as soon as possible, and violence was to be the spark that would trigger a mass revolution.[52]

Other records from the trial seem to suggest that before he was sentenced to death Gudō had renounced anarchism. In a record dated October 27, 1910, Gudō is reported as saying that during his detention in a Yokohama prison, "in silent reflection I have come to realize that anarchism has internal contradictions and cannot possibly be realized in practice; therefore, I have abandoned that ideology."[53] Previously, he had said that "I regret having until now advocated anarchism,"[54] and "I came to understand that anarchism is an evil-spreading ideology."[55] Indeed, a source explicitly lists Gudō's name among those of "people who have abandoned their ideology."[56] Another record, supposedly reporting Gudō's words, contains some possible explanations:

We anarchists too, because of a certain kind of desire, plot a violent movement; but even if we succeeded in overthrowing the present ruler, a different kind of ruler would necessarily come; this is why I came to understand that what Kropotkin calls the anarchical condition cannot possibly be realized in society.[57]

Of course, one has to be careful when interpreting sudden ideological conversions that take place in prison under threat of the death penalty. What is certain is that Gudō was unable to propose a clear blueprint for revolutionary activity. *Museifu kyōsan kakumei* and the two translations of anarchist tracts he published do indeed contain appeals to violent, direct action, but the gist of their political praxis is constituted by exhortations to acquire consciousness of social mechanisms, participate in radical movements, and form labor unions in order to mobilize large numbers of individuals against the state. In this respect, Gudō was probably closer than we may have thought to such late-Tokugawa reformist activists as Ninomiya Sontoku (1787–1856), who emphasized cooperative organization.[58]

In addition, the rejection of military conscription was in line not only with contemporary socialist thought but also, and especially, with the Buddhist precept against taking life. Furthermore, the idea that one's consumption should be directly related to one's actual labor was in accordance with Zen teachings about self-reliance.[59]

However, Gudō was also aware of the massive anti-revolutionary propaganda and the severe repression of labor movements by the state. Yet his exhortations to provide strong moral examples and to be ready for self-sacrifice were obviously not enough for a revolutionary movement to succeed. Indeed, even his most developed political text, *Heibon no jikaku*, is striking for its lack of specific plans for action. Concerning the actual method to implement common ownership in industry, Gudō disarmingly writes that "it is conceivable that both capitalists and workers who have acquired consciousness will find the necessary clues and start the whole process."[60] In other words, "clues" will be discovered only after the agents involved acquire consciousness, as a result of a process that is largely left to individual sensibility and disposition. In this respect, Gudō seems to have believed that powerful examples set by a few heroic individuals might function as catalysts for awareness. In his eyes, direct action was also an exemplary action aimed at awakening the masses and leading them toward revolutionary consciousness.

In this, he was following Kropotkin's message that there are people in society who have acquired consciousness and they will serve as the sparks that trigger revolution, but their actions might also require self-sacrifice.[61] Interestingly, this attitude is not in contradiction to the Japanese tradition of righteous revolt dating back to at least the Edo period; indeed, in what is perhaps Gudō's last writing, he mentions Śākyamuni, the Greek philosopher Diogenes,[62] and Jesus Christ, but also famous Edo-period champions of social virtue such as Sakura Sōgorō and Ōshio Heihachirō, as noble examples of self-sacrifice. We will discuss this in some detail in the next chapter.

Chapter 3

Gudō's Intellectual Bricolage

At the time when Gudō was active, anarchism was a new and largely unprecedented political doctrine in Japan. Whereas ideas of socialism and communism were first introduced to the country by Katō Hiroyuki in his *Shinsei taii* (1870),[1] anarchism began in earnest when Kōtoku Shūsui returned to Japan from his stay in California in 1906. In the early Meiji period there had been discussions about the terrorist activities of the Russian nihilists (or populists, *narodniki*) and their suppression, and in the eyes of many people, the anarchists were closely related to the nihilists. Authorities and conservative people saw anarchism as a dangerous threat to their political control, but many intellectuals found it an exciting field of new ideas and practices. The first systematic introduction of anarchism in Japan was in a book, *Kinsei museifushugi* (*Modern Anarchism*), by Kemuyama Sentarō, published in 1902, which became influential for the development of Japanese anarchism; its readers included Kōtoku Shūsui, Kanno Sugako (also known as Kanno Suga), Ōsugi Sakae, and Miyashita Takichi. This book was very critical of anarchism, called *kyomushugi* (nihilism), which was presented explicitly as a "social disease" (*shakai no shippei*). However, Kemuyama was also able to see in anarchism a natural and fundamental human desire for freedom based on individualism.[2]

Because of anarchism's novelty, authors attempted to make it more familiar by finding precedents in the Japanese tradition. For example, Tarui Tōkichi (1850–1922), one of the founders in 1882 of the first socialist party in Japan, the Tōyō shakaitō, compared anarchist nihilism to Daoist and Buddhist doctrines.[3] More generally, progressive authors identified the Tokugawa thinker Andō Shōeki (1703–1762) as a Japanese anarchist. However, the role played by Kōtoku Shūsui and, through him, Piotr Kropotkin was paramount for the early anarchist movement in Japan, and for Uchiyama Gudō in particular.[4] Especially important was Kropotkin's book *The Conquest of Bread*, published in French in 1892 and in English in 1906, and translated into Japanese by Kōtoku and others.

As we have thus far seen, Gudō was attempting to mobilize the intellectual resources that were available to him in order to "domesticate," as it were, anarchism to his personal situation and the social condition of the time, as well as to formulate a blueprint for concrete action aimed at the liberation of the commoners, not as an exercise in abstract philosophy. We have also seen that it is doubtful he succeeded in such a formulation. These two dimensions, however, were not unrelated; in fact, in a very Buddhist fashion, Gudō assumes as a starting point the development of awareness of social mechanisms and one's position and possibilities within them. We should also add that Gudō, mostly unencumbered by ideological positions and pressures to conform to foreign models and party authority, was more free than others to develop his thought in original ways.

Morinaga Eizaburō has suggested that in Gudō's time, Buddhism lacked the force to correct the inequalities in the real world; the image of equality Gudō saw in the collective life of Chinese monks could not be extended to secular society. He therefore decided to employ socialism, especially anarchism, in order to bridge Buddhist spirituality and social revolutionary activism. For Gudō, in this sense, at least, Buddhism and anarchism were mutually reinforcing rather than conflicting and mutually exclusive.[5]

On the other hand, we cannot ignore the fact that Gudō never tried to relate Buddhism to anarchism in his public writings. Certainly he was aware of the conservative nature of the official Buddhist discourse of the time, and perhaps, progressive ideology was alien from the ways in which Buddhism was commonly understood. In any case, Gudō was not striving for a socialist form of Buddhism but rather was engaged in a socialist/anarchist movement as a Buddhist.

The historian of Japanese anarchism Ōsawa Masamichi has argued that attempts to combine anarchism and Buddhism by a few countryside intellectuals of good conscience, such as Gudō, ended in a twofold failure; namely, they were unable to either transform traditional thought in progressive terms or to promote the acceptance of new progressive ideologies from abroad. The main problem with Gudō's efforts and those of his fellows, according to Ōsawa, was that they attempted to bring together Buddhism and anarchism, two radically different systems of thought, only on the basis of superficial similarities, through a traditional logic of amalgamation (kongōshugi).[6]

More recently, Sueki Fumihiko has attempted to counter Ōsawa's criticism, positing that precisely this kind of confrontation with and amalgamation of different intellectual and ideological systems that took place at a grass-roots level had strong possibilities to assimilate new ideas at a local, practical level (and not just in terms of an abstract history of ideas).[7] Sueki does not indicate the actual ways in which such practical assimilation took place in Gudō's case, however.

We have seen that Gudō's attempt to bridge Buddhist doctrines and concrete social action, which aimed not only to improve living conditions for the poor and working-class people but also and especially to create an anarchist society of free individuals and communities, was expressed through the soteriological and eschatological image of paradise (*tengoku*).[8] The choice of terminology is significant, because the Japanese term *tengoku* refers to the Christian paradise and not to the Buddhist realms of bliss, normally expressed by terms such as *gokuraku* (land of supreme bliss) or *jōdo* (pure land).

Other scholars have pointed to the presence of Christian elements in Gudō's writings, without attempting to explain them, unless as rudimentary attempts at amalgamation based on superficial similarities.[9] I suggest three different but related possible interpretations. In the first place, Christianity in Meiji Japan was closely connected with the development of the socialist movement, and some of these associations may have influenced the terminology of discourses of liberation. Second, the discourse of international socialist and anarchist movements already contained many eschatological images and themes, including a secularist appropriation of Jesus Christ as a fighter for the liberation of the oppressed; thus, it is not surprising that Gudō refers to Jesus in this way.[10] Finally, the Buddhist notion of a Pure Land had come to be associated with specific teachings, in particular to a postmortem realm of the dead, and as such was hardly appealing for a revolutionary attempt to radically transform contemporary society.[11]

We should also consider the possibility that the Christian-derived term *tengoku* was, in Gudō's use, an attempt to give theoretical depth to late-Tokugawa peasant revolts aimed at the radical transformation of society and the entire world, known as *yonaoshi* (lit., "rectification of the world"). In this respect, the movement called Eejanaika comes to mind, with its complete rejection of authority, social conventions and rules, and its transgressive, playful components. Eejanaika began in 1867 in Nagoya and within a few months it spread in many parts of Japan before it was severely repressed by the authorities.[12] We should note, however, that Gudō's writings display very little playfulness, and emphasize instead a clear sense of class identity, awareness of mechanisms of exploitation, and the importance of work and personal responsibility.

Shinto, especially in its folkloric components, was notably absent in Gudō's public writings. Instead, he wrote a scathing criticism of State Shinto (*kokka shintō*) and its imperial cult, the sacred ideology of the modern Japanese state.[13] He openly questioned the divinity of the Japanese emperor: "The boss of this government, the emperor, is not the son of a god, as the schoolteachers deceivingly tell you"; the emperor "has been tormented by his guards outside, and inside he has been treated as a toy by his own servants." In fact,

> The ancestors of the present emperor came from a remote corner of Kyushu; murdering and stealing, they eventually killed one of their fellow brigands, Nagasunebiko; it's as if Kumasaka Chōhan or Shuten Dōji from Ōeyama had won.[14]

Despite this, "You are taught that you must work hard and serve the descendant of thieves who wears the mask of a god."[15] As we can see, Gudō did not hesitate to call the emperor the "descendant of thieves and murderers," and to compare him to two evil figures of premodern popular culture, the demon Shuten Dōji and the brigand Kumasaka Chōhan. Gudō even saw the emperor as the person most responsible for the wretched conditions of the Japanese proletariat:

> [B]ecause of him (the emperor), you tenant farmers have troubles every single day getting enough food to eat in spite of your earnest labor! They say that Japan is the land of the gods, but you tenant farmers have little to be thankful for that.[16]

Instead, "what the old sages called paradise (*tengoku*) or the land of the gods (*shinkoku*)" is a society in which "all human beings must secure their clothing and food through their own labor."[17] Gudō thus appropriated and reversed dominant ideas of Japan as a sacred country, the "land of the gods" (*shinkoku*); in his interpretation, *shinkoku* is a synonym of paradise (*tengoku*), not in a religious way but rather as a realized anarchist society in which there is no private property and all people live out of their own labor.

We should note here another possible component of Gudō's anarchism, namely, the Daoist tradition.[18] The *Laozi* presents a vision of self-governed village communities attentive to the happiness and self-realization of each individual. The *Zhuangzi* further develops those elements in a clearer libertarian direction, even describing the predatory nature of the state and its rulers: "A petty thief is put in jail. A great brigand becomes a ruler of a state." It is no accident that one of the leading libertarian thinkers,

Murray Rothbard, has characterized Zhuangzi as being "perhaps the world's first anarchist."[19]

Another theme that resonates with a Daoist outlook is the rejection of ordinary morals, which are deeply steeped in Confucian norms and sanctioned by the dominant classes. A short essay Gudō published in January 1908 in the magazine *Sekai fujin* opens with the words:

> To tell you with all sincerity what my beliefs are, if we delete from the dictionary of ethics the little words filiality (*kō*), loyalty to one's superiors (*chū*), and also chastity (*tei*), the world will see heaven (*tengoku*) for the first time.[20]

Here, Gudō was rejecting the Confucian principles more directly related to social hierarchy and subjugation, while implicitly preserving values such as humaneness and friendship.[21]

Indeed, we find very little Confucian influence (at least, normative versions of Confucianism) in Gudō's writings; references to Confucius are mostly popular proverbs, such as "if one has heard the Way in the morning, it is all right to die in the evening" and "sacrifice yourself in order to realize the virtue of humaneness."[22] However, a possible Confucian element in Gudō might be represented by a link (albeit indirect) with Wang Yangming's thought, especially in its emphasis on direct action and its ties with the Japanese tradition of righteous revolt (and politically motivated self-sacrifice), from Sakura Sōgorō (1605?–1653) and Ōshio Heihachirō (1793–1837) to Mishima Yukio (1925–1970).[23] The problem with this tradition is that action was primarily a manifestation of individual morality and almost never became the seed for widespread social change. In this sense, Gudō is probably another character in the long Japanese drama about the *beau geste* as an end in itself, what has been called the "nobility of failure"[34]—which is also, at the same time, a "failure of nobility" (as noble intentions).

It is within this context of voluntarism that we should read Gudō's emphasis on self-sacrifice, on giving up one's life for revolution, and his quest for a sense of joyful self-fulfillment that characterize his last, unpublished writings. If this is indeed the case, then his was really a creative and original attempt at formulating a modern praxis of liberation that combined traditional elements with new, Western ideas. If such an experiment had not been violently interrupted by state repression (which turned it into another case in the "nobility of failure" series), it might have taken more definite forms and spread among the Japanese society. On the other hand, we should also be aware that the Confucian tradition in Japan in the Tokugawa period was far from unified and that

Confucian thought at times became the catalyst for innovative discourses and attempts at social change, as also indicated by the long tradition of peasant revolts based on Confucianism. We have already men-
tioned the figure of Andō Shōeki, who has been indicated by many as
the pioneer of Japanese anarchism. More to the point, radical authors
such as Kōtoku Shūsui and Sakai Toshihiko both claimed that their own
conversion to socialism was the result of their study of Confucianism—
a further indication that Confucianism was understood in different, and
at times unorthodox ways, and that people tried to relate new western
ideas about socialism (and later, communism and anarchism) to their
own political and intellectual backgrounds.[35]

We can perhaps find another key to understand Gudō's thought in the
late nineteenth-century Romantic narrative elements that pervade his
writings, in particular, themes such as the revolutionary hero ready to
sacrifice himself in order to free the subjugated masses, revolutionary society as a sort of paradise on earth, and a combination of mysticism and
utilitarianism. How these themes spread in Japan and what were their
larger cultural effects will have to be addressed elsewhere, but it is perhaps possible to indicate their starting point in late Tokugawa and early
Meiji awareness of the French Revolution. This epochal event alerted the
Japanese about the possibility of radical changes in government and culture, and brought with it new ideas about freedom.[36] Another, certainly
more influential source of images about popular heroes fighting despotic authorities in favor of the subaltern masses can be found in popular
European literature from the second half of the nineteenth century.[37]

From this brief discussion we can see the complex intertextual and
intellectual background of Gudō's thought, in which the global discourse of anarchism intersected the popular Japanese intellectual tradition.[38] Germaine Hoston has argued that "In Japan . . . anarchism
emerged out of an anti-Westernism and an aspiration to return to traditional values."[39] In particular,

> Kōtoku and his followers also experienced a deep yearning for the restoration
> of what they believed to be traditional Japanese virtues, many of which were
> expressed in the *kokutai* (national polity) of the organic community itself.[40]

In Gudō's writings, anti-Westernism and Japanese traditionalism are
not as prominent as his emphasis on internationalism, world peace, and
marginalized (non-mainstream) aspects of Japanese thought, such as
Buddhist democratic tendencies, critiques of Confucian morality, and
autonomous village communal practices.

Part Two

Translations of Uchiyama Gudō's Main Works

"*Vademecum* for the Soldiers in the Imperial Army"

from *L'anarchie*, translated by Ōsugi Sakae

A message to the new conscripts:

In our country of Japan, which, as people keep saying everywhere in the land, is the best country in the world, in a few days you all will be separated from the warm embrace of your parents, siblings, and loved ones, and for three years you will be thrown in that jail called military service.

The concept of state has already been carved deeply into your brains by the family and at school. Every day you are told that the peoples with different traditions, habits, and languages, who live outside of that hypothetical line called frontier, are your enemies. Now, with the excuse of protecting your country, you are forced to pay a blood tribute to learn that most shameful thing, namely, how to become a murderer, which will make of you devils among human beings.

However, if the army exists only to protect our country of Japan, why isn't the army only deployed at the borders or along the coast? Why is it also deployed deeply inside the national territory?

In truth, the army has been regularly used to preserve the social order of the state. To put it more bluntly, when the people arise in order to demand their just rights, the army is deployed to repress the people so as to protect the wallets of the classes in power.

The bourgeois economist J. B. Say said: "The army, far from protecting the independence of a country, is in fact the cause of its destruction."[1] These are words that need to be deeply pondered today as well.

But you, what are you taught when you wear that ridiculous uniform? You are simply forced to give up your rationality and sensibility and to acquire a blind spirit of class submission. In other words, you are taught that whenever there is an order from your superiors you have to execute it immediately without complaint.

In addition to a feeling of enmity toward foreigners, they also teach you that people who have ideas against the government, the law, and the orders [they receive from their superiors], are all bandits, even though they were born in your same country.

In this way, they take away from you critical thinking and freedom, and you will end up becoming murderers—the claws and fangs of authoritarianism.

You will also become temporary military police and will be deployed to defend the capitalists. You will be deployed to suppress strikes. You will be deployed to obstruct citizens' gatherings. Sometimes, when following the outrageous orders of your superiors, you will end up shooting your own parents, siblings, and friends.

All wars are crimes. Because they are always fought only for the benefit of the profiteers and the speculators, we say to you: don't become sacrificial lambs! Stop turning yourselves into miserable slaves! Proclaim that you want nothing to do with the butchers! Then, engage yourselves in protecting your own lives!

The state is sweet to the rich and bitter to the poor. You are to sacrifice two or three years of your youth to protect the property of the rich and the aristocracy.

Don't forget, when you are deployed to suppress strikes, that you are confronting your own brothers!

Don't forget, when you are deployed outside our national borders, that you are sacrificing yourselves for the bottomless greed of bankers and speculators! When you get sick or when you are injured, when you return home, the state will be like an ogress stepmother toward you.

These are the reasons why we antimilitarists have decided to counter the war declaration with general desertion.

Break your own chains by yourselves! Begin to love humanity! If it's necessary to shed your blood, do it on behalf of your own happiness and freedom!

The imminent revolution will establish anarchist communism, that is, it will create the most free society, both politically and economically. Your general desertion is the primary factor for its success. Engage yourselves in it!

Conscripts—

It breaks our heart when we think about the future of our wives and children and of our white-haired parents. Stop talking about that glory nonsense! We go toward our death without saying anything, with our eyes closed, hiding our tears, just because of social obligations toward the country.[2]

"Anarchism and the Repudiation of Morals"

by Max Baginsky

Property is theft. The state and its laws are protectors of stolen articles.
Ethics and religion are clerks for thieves.

There is only one thing in this world more unjust than the desire to rule over people, namely, the intention to subject oneself to it.[1]

At first sight it would seem that the rulers and the rich today have immense power and that their position in society is extremely solid, but in fact they are facing extremely difficult problems and they are in great distress over how to solve them. What are these problems? Their privileges are already in a critical situation; how can they be protected? The people's trust in the "state" is decreasing every day; how can it be maintained? And finally, how can they bring comfort to the hearts of the people who are more and more suspicious of the degeneration and the crimes of the rich and the powerful?

Originally, the most essential thing for rulers is the absolute trust and respect from the people; without these, it is impossible to rule even just for one day, and obviously the government is not safe. Until now, they have used the church, the schools, the family system, and various other institutions for their own interests. Thanks to the ignorance, stupidity, and character of the people, they have been able to stick deeply inside the people's guts the very unnatural teachings of respect for authority and love for the state.

Throughout the premodern era, it was not too difficult for the rulers to implement such stratagems. In the modern era, however, the invention of the press, despite its great power to widely spread national prejudices and class falsities, at the same time is also effective in spreading revolutionary free thinking. Thanks to it, this heroic and indomitable new spirit [of ours] has been awakening the people from their old delusions and has enabled them to think with their own brains.

No matter how stupid a person is, if he thinks only a little, he will immediately have doubts; he is now able to ask questions such as: What is generally called "truth"—is it really the truth? What government officials, lackey scholars, and priests praise in unison as "justice"—is it really just?

At last, the silly era is now way past when Buddhist priests and emperors used to divine the destiny of the people they ruled by looking at the shadows of birds or by listening to the sounds of animals. At that time, the people paid the utmost respect to imperial messages and oracles, but today no one takes those things seriously. Not only that: Today, people have come to realize that they cannot trust at all even the representatives and legislators they have themselves elected, because of their corruption and degeneration. So, the human race, after wandering in the darkness for a very long time, has gradually acquired consciousness and now realizes that politics, religion, and social institutions are mere bridles created by rulers and capitalists to defend their own interests within the established "order" and to enchain the poor and the workers and take away from them the products of their own labor.

However, because the people's consciousness is very dangerous for the rulers, the latter always have to find new methods and tools to keep the people in a condition of slavery. Until now, religion has been a very powerful tool for this purpose, but today at last it is no longer as effective as in the past. If we take a superficial look at society, we see many temples and churches scattered here and there, like the scars of smallpox that make ugly the face of a person; they are traces of past superstitions that still remain in today's world. Even merchants and politicians who follow the most recent trends still offer prayers to the gods before engaging in their activities. When gamblers go to their gaming joints, they make offerings to the gods and pray for their good fortune; it is like the pirates of Italy who, before going to "work," offer many candles to Santa Marie's (sic) altar so that they can get a large booty.

Setting these things aside, religion, in fact, has already lost completely its influence today, both in economic and social terms, and no longer has the power to promote good and repel evil. Thus, this omnipotent and supremely good god is fooled and exploited by sly people, like a simple member of a trade association. This kind of pious people come up with various sly stratagems to swindle simpletons and strip them of the fruits of their labor; they hurt them, they murder them; they do all sorts of evil things in the world, and slyly give the responsibility for these crimes to others, and prophesy that their own soul will go to god's place.

In this way, religion today has no power to prevent the rich from oppressing the poor. However, the impotence and the defects of religion are now widely known; as a consequence, it is now difficult to stop the revolt of the masses against the social systems, and therefore religion no longer has the authority to keep the masses forever in a slave-like state of subjugation. Thus, the oppressors are hard-pressed to find something else instead of religion, and what they ended up finding is morals.

These moral precepts, like religion, are essentially something that has coercive authority to order "do this, don't do that" [or "do good, don't do evil"], but these orders issue forth not, like in old times, from the mouth of a god or the emperor, but from some stuff called inner voice, moral conscience, duty, etc. In other words, the only difference is that, whereas before oppression came from the outside, now shackles are on the inside.

The "chains of religion" that shackled human actions against god, the king, the aristocracy, and the rich have grown weaker every day and now have almost disappeared; to save the situation, the invention of a moral reformation to destroy humankind's natural desire and the masses' requests for consciousness is, perhaps, an unavoidable move for the powerful and the classes that wield authority. Recently, education and publishing have expanded enormously the number of moral duties and ask of the people many difficult tasks in the attempt to uproot continuing human progress toward consciousness. The professors of morals have become oppressors even more stubborn and merciless than judges and priests, and have imposed moral restrictions on all everyday human activities; they have even issued moral laws limiting science, philosophy, and art.

This morality has even imposed strict prohibitions upon the free union of man and woman, and has succeeded in producing forced marriage, prostitution, and rampant venereal diseases. According to these moral teachings, all men and women are forbidden to freely satisfy their physical needs if they are not "officially married."

In contemporary society, however, economic scarcity, that is, poverty, is an obstacle and in many cases people cannot marry according to those moral principles. Thus, at the age in which passions are strongest and sex is most needed, the only paths left to young men and women are a sad life of solitude, prostitution, and debauchery. These three things are the precious gifts given to us by economic structure and moral precepts.

Against all this, we reject any and all shackles and constraints imposed upon the free activities of human beings in politics, economics, society, and all other fields. Therefore, we strenuously oppose all tools, such as morals, [that are] used to oppress the weak and the poor.

Recently, during a strike by the street cleaners in New York, journalists and government officers have harshly criticized them, saying that the cleaners were neglecting their responsibilities and disregarding their moral duties toward the city. However, is cleaning carefully the streets (in particular, cleaning very well the neighborhoods of the rich) really an obvious duty for workers like the street cleaners, who work in terrible conditions for cheap wages? If so, this is a duty that is valid only among that clique of fine gentlemen, a moral that is not worth a penny for the workers.

Bourgeois morality tells the workers to endure their condition of need and poverty so that the rich can go on forever with their lazy lives as parasites.

In this way, so-called morality is a very lucrative business for the rich and the exploiters and, at the same time, is the harshest life sentence for the poor. If we, the poor and the weak, did not have the fortunate chance to commit immoral acts, there would be no hope for us to avoid our painful burden.

People also say: when one does his job truthfully he will experience "moral satisfaction" in that job.

We can hear a voice here saying "labor is sacred." However, this is just hypocrisy. For a person with the true spirit of autonomy and independence it is absolutely impossible to experience "moral satisfaction" in a slave-like wage job. On the contrary, he will feel such toil to be the most unbearable humiliation and it would be impossible for him not to revolt against the present system that turns him into a sort of machine accumulating wealth for others. Thus, if there are people who do not manifest their sense of injustice against the shackles and oppression they are subjected to, well, these people are born slaves and have completely lost the spirit and the energy of men.

Moreover, current morality strongly prohibits the appropriation of other people's property. For example, the moral duty of a poor person without a house to live in is that of quietly walking by the mansions of the rich. If he sneaks inside a house and rests his tired body for a while, they immediately call him a criminal, treat him as a different kind of human being, and throw him in jail.

This morality is unnatural, inhumane, and antisocial. Today's moralists scream "Thief!" when a hungry beggar takes a slice of bread, but every day they take away more than half of the workers' production. They kneel down before the "successful capitalists" and praise their large thefts without reflecting on their own actions. Thus, morality is just a synonym for hypocrisy, and the free-thinking man should not have respect for it.

Anarchism is a revolt against violent attacks targeting peaceful individuals.

The crimes an individual should not commit, should not be committed by the government either.

Everything the government can do to help the people, can be done by the people themselves without the help of the government.

The only protection needed by honest people is the protection of their property from the brigands called the state.

Today's education is a practice to make people at the same time subservient and submissive toward their superiors and arrogant and insolent toward their inferiors.

Among all forms of polity, the ugliest and most repressive is the representative system, which allows a part of the people free dominion over all the others.

"Anarchist Communist Revolution"
(*Museifu kyōsan kakumei*)

(In Commemoration of Imprisonment)

Why is Life So Hard for Tenant Farmers?

You tenant farmers, you who produce food, the most important thing for human beings, the one thing we cannot do without, you all, since the old times of your ancestors, have worked hard to produce food, this most essential thing of all, but every year ends in scarcity for you. What sort of bad luck is this?

Is it because of what the Buddhists call bad retribution from your past lives? But seriously, folks, if today, in our world of the twentieth century, you are still deceived by this kind of superstition, you will really end up like cows and horses. Are you folks happy about being still poor every single year and complaining that what you have is not enough? Suppose that during the cold winter you could take your aging parents to Zushi, or Kamakura, or Numazu, or Hayama, because they hate the cold and so that they can take some rest in one of those places—in that case you could still bear your situation. Again, if in the hot summer you could take you ailing wife and children to Hakone or Nikkō,[1] where they could find relief from the heat; even if this year you don't have enough, you could still find some comfort. Suppose that, in order to send your eldest son to Germany to study, his little brother to the university, and your daughter to a women's high school, you had to sell a hundred hectares of forest, or pledge fifty hectares of arable land as collateral for a loan; even so, counting on the good things that await you in the future because of that investment, your conversations with your wife in bed would not be so gloomy and painful.

However, when you folks complain, all year long, every year, that you don't have enough, it's certainly not because you allow yourselves such luxuries. You don't buy a new kimono just because it's New Year or *O-bon;*[2] in our twentieth-century world civilization, architectural technology has made many advances, but in spite of that your houses haven't changed

45

for a long time; in fact, your houses are exactly the same as they were five hundred or one thousand years ago. But all this is quite obvious; in order to buy a kimono, you have to give money to a mercer; for the house, you have to pay the wages of the carpenters. But you folks, unfortunately, don't have such money. That is why your kimonos are always in rags and your houses are like animals' burrows.

On the other hand, since you produce food, do you eat food of the best quality? Of course not. The best rice is taken by the landowner, and you have to eat millet or barley, still you work much more than the land-lords and the merchants. In spite of that, every year you must suffer penury; this is the tenant farmers' fate.

Why is it so? There is a song saying,

> *Why are you so poor? If you want to know the reason I will tell you:*
> *That's because there is vermin that sucks people's blood;*
> *They are the emperor, the rich, and the big landowners.*[3]

Folks, try to think. Of what you produce with your sweat all year long, half is taken by a thief called the landlord; with the half that's left, you buy sake, soy sauce, salt, and manure. But on that sake, on that manure, on everything, nothing excluded, there are taxes—money that is taken by that big thief called the government. On top of that, other thieves called merchants make their own profit. That's why folks like you tenant farmers, who don't own your land, will never be able to avoid poverty throughout your life, no matter how hard and earnestly you work.

And it could still be acceptable, if that were all. If you have a son, after you raise him in poverty, how glad you are that he can finally help you making even just one more ridge in the field, so that you can hope to be able to just barely avoid borrowing money. But at that point, when your son is twenty-one, he is taken by the army, no matter how you hate that. Then, for three years, you have to send him money, while—and you don't even want to hear about that—he is trained to become a murder-er. Then, if there is a war, he is forced to go to a bloody place, where he either kills people or is himself killed.

There are even fathers who, during the three years their son is taken away from them by the army, are forced to go begging with their wives and other children. There are so many young people in the army who, because their families are poor and cannot send them money, are hazed by their senior comrades, and end up hanging themselves, or jumping into a river, or killing themselves on a railway.

This is how they harass you, you tenant farmers! You folks wake up early in the morning with the birds and work until dark, yet cannot get rid of poverty.

Why does all this happen? We are all born as human beings, but if you are born in a family of landowners or rich people you can play at school or abroad until you are twenty-four, twenty-five or even thirty; then, when you go back home, you can escape from the summer heat to a cool place, and you [can] build a house on the warm coast and spend winter there leisurely. Isn't it so? They wear silk kimonos without having to pick up even one single leaf of mulberry, and live in luxury drinking sake and eating meat as they please. They enjoy themselves without doing anything all their life. You folks perhaps don't know it, but the big landlords and the rich spend 2,000 or 3,000 yen for one person to enjoy their summer month in Nikkō or Hakone, don't they? I mean, 3,000 yen! There's no way you folks can make that much money even if you work all day, without resting and without eating much, from when you are twenty until when you are fifty. And those people don't even have to join the army.

Tenant farmers! I'm sure you'd like to live a life of luxury like those rich people and big landowners. To have fun and eat good food once in a while. But you can't do that, because you hold on to some particular superstitions. And because since the old time of your ancestors you have treasured these superstitions, you cannot even dream of a life of luxury like the landowners and the rich enjoy. But if you folks listen to what we have to tell you and just give up those superstitions now, you will truly become free men able to live in comfort.

However, if you give up these superstitions the emperor and the rich will no longer be able to afford their own lives of ease and luxury, and so from ancient times the emperors and the daimyos have been cheating you by telling you that these superstitions are precious and essential things. Therefore, you should not forget that, for you folks, today's emperor and ministers, and in the past the Tokugawa and the daimyos from the ancient time of your ancestors, are your great enemies, against whom you should have piled up many grudges.

Even today, in the Meiji era, it is the same thing. The government, using everyone from university professors down to elementary schoolteachers, is doing everything in its power to prevent you from giving up these superstitions. And you folks, you are thankful for that. That is why you won't be able to get rid of poverty for all your life—no, not just your own life, but also the lives of your descendants.

Now, what are these superstitions that schoolteachers teach you and your children? A superstition is a wrong idea that one holds precious like a sacred thing. I will tell you later why you people have been holding on to these wrong ideas since the remote past; now, let me tell you what these wrong ideas, these superstitions, are.

- Since you are graciously given the chance to cultivate the fields by the landowner, you must pay him land rent (*shōsakumai*) as a token of your gratitude.

- Precisely because there is government, we peasants can work in peace. We must pay our taxes as a token of gratitude for that.

- If our country did not have enough armaments, we peasants would end up being killed by the foreigners. Therefore, we must send our young, strong boys into the army.

This is it. Because these three wrong ideas have penetrated deeply into your minds, you do not protest against paying land rent, taxes, or sending your sons to the army, no matter how poor you are. If someone told you, it's OK not to pay your land rent, it's OK not to pay your taxes, it's OK not to send your beloved son to the army, you would think such a person is a rebel or a traitor to the country and you would not listen or read about such ideas, even though these ideas are in fact meant for your freedom and for improving your life. This is what I would like you to think and read carefully about the most.

Now, why do some people say it's OK not to pay rent to the landowners? Well, the fields that you tenant farmers cultivate—try to leave them alone, from spring until fall, without plowing, sowing, and fertilizing them. When the fall comes, there will be not a single grain of rice; in the summer, no one will be able to harvest even half a grain of barley. If you think of it in this way, one immediately understands. Rice ripens in the fall, and barley in the summer, only because you tenant farmers work without rest all year round. If you think of it in this way, the rice and the barley that result from your own work, all belong to you tenant farmers. Why in the world should one give half of it to the landowner? That's nonsense!

The land originally existed in nature and our ancestors developed it so that they could grow food. Why is it that he who takes possession of the things he himself has harvested after cultivating the land is called a rebel?

For a long time you tenant farmers have been robbed by the landowners, but now, right now, if you awaken from your delusion, you can finally take your revenge not only by not paying your annual rent, you also have the right to take back the barley and the money accumulated in the landowner's storehouse. It's definitely not thievery to take away everything from inside the landowner's storehouse. On the contrary, to recover what has been taken away from you tenant farmers, and from all of us, over a long time is an honorable endeavor.

Next, why is it OK not to pay taxes to the government? Tenant farmers, there is no need for complicated arguments. You tenant farmers, just how is your life better thanks to the existence of the government? If there is just one little thing for which you are grateful to His Excellency, Mr. Government, tell me. Since of old, it is said that you cannot win against crying babies and the land steward. Indeed, the exercise of odious oppression is the job of those in power, isn't it? You tenant farmers work hard and pay your taxes honestly in order to support those hideous people, and as a consequence you remain poor. This is the maximum of stupidity.

Folks, let's stop paying taxes to the stupid government, and let's ruin those hideous people as soon as we can! Then, let's take back the wealth that the government has stolen from us over a long time through force and oppression, from the time of our ancestors, and let's keep it in common! This is your natural right, and the people who love justice should actively rebel against the government for freedom and a better life for all.

To destroy the present government and establish a free country without an emperor is not treason but an action appropriate to heroes who love justice. Why is this so? The boss of this government, the emperor, is not the son of a god, as the schoolteachers deceivingly tell you. The ancestors of the present emperor came from a remote corner of Kyushu; murdering and stealing, they eventually killed one of their fellow brigands, Nagasunebiko;[4] it's as if Kumasaka Chōhan or Shuten Dōji from Ōeyama had won.[5] It is easy to understand that the emperor is not a god if you just think about it. One might think that he is actually a god just because [his dynasty] has continued for 2,500 years, but in fact for all this time he has been tormented by his guards[6] on the outside, and inside he has been treated as a toy by his own servants.

Even now in this Meiji era, it's just the same. The emperor, they say, has been suffering because of internal politics and international relations. However, one reaps as one has sown, and this suffering of the emperor's is all of his own making and is none of our concerns. Rather, because of him, you tenant farmers have troubles every single day getting enough food to eat in spite of your earnest labor! They say that Japan is the land of the gods, but you tenant farmers have little to be thankful for that.

That bunch of wimps, university professors and scholars, cannot say or write about all these obvious things; instead, they tell the people hundreds of lies to the point that they end up deceiving themselves! Elementary schoolteachers are especially at pains to teach about being grateful to the emperor, but they are gradually getting better at telling lies, and every year on the occasion of the three great holidays, they teach you and your children, looking as if they didn't know [any] better, that the emperor is the son of the gods. You are taught that you must work hard and serve this descendant of thieves who wears the mask of a god, and because of that, you folks will forever be unable to get rid of poverty. After hearing all this, even the most patient among you would certainly decide to join the [revolutionary] movement, even at the cost of your own lives, to take back what has been stolen from all of you.

Tenant farmers! Because of these old superstitions, you have believed that if the country has no army, the common people will not survive. Of course, both in the past and in the present, it is obvious that, if war breaks out, a country without an army will be destroyed by a country that has one. However, war happens because there are those great thieves called emperors and governments. Isn't war a fight between one government and another? It boils down to this: because thieves fight among themselves, the common people suffer. If we eliminate the thief called government, war will disappear. If there is no more war, then there is no need to send your beloved sons to the army. It's as simple as that!

Now, all this means that the fastest way to eliminate that great thief called government is to stop paying land rent to the landowners, paying taxes, and sending your sons into the army.

There are several methods to put this ideology into practice. First, you tenant farmers, even just ten or twenty among you, should form a labor union and put these things into practice—namely, don't pay land rent to the landowner, don't pay taxes to the government, and don't send your sons into the army. If you begin acting in this way, and since many people love justice, your movement will spread from one village to one district, from one district to one prefecture, and eventually from Japan to the whole world, and at that point the ideal land of anarchist communism, where all are free and live a comfortable life, will be realized.

Nothing can be realized without sacrifice. If you want to join us, for the sake of justice, let's start this movement even at the risk of our own lives!

On June 22, 1908, in the capital of the Empire of Japan, I and some ten comrades raised the red flag of anarchist communism and declared our resistance against the emperor, and on August 29 of the same year we were convicted.

I printed this booklet to commemorate the imprisonment of Ōsugi Sakae, Arahata Shōzō, Satō Satori, Momose Susumi, Utsunomiya Takuji, Morioka Eiji, Sakai Toshihiko, Muraki Genjirō,[7] Ōsuga Sato, Yamakawa Hitoshi, Ogure Rei,[8] and Tokunaga Yasunosuke.

This booklet should be used by the few comrades in the capital to continue to spread our message during the absence of our imprisoned comrades, until they get out of prison in one to four years.

Those of you who, after reading this booklet, understand that the coming revolution is for the realization of anarchist communism, please send letters or postcards to the comrades in prison. This is their only consolation, but it is also a gospel to study the courage of the fighting heroes.

Please address the letters to the comrades in prison.

> To: Mr. or Ms. So-and-so, Inmate in Ushigome Ichigaya Tokyo Prison, Tokyo City

> Clearly write also the name and address of the sender.

This booklet awakens you from your long-lasting superstitious dreams, and urges you to participate in our revolution that will take place in the near future; the content of this booklet has to be spread widely and deeply, so that people do not misunderstand our reasoning. I hope this message will be spread to as many people as possible, people who will not be afraid of even throwing dynamite for the cause of anarchist communism. I also hope that those people who, after reading this booklet, do not agree with us, will still think seriously about whether our present society is a just society, and whether our ideals will perfect this society or not.

"Common Consciousness"
(*Heibon no jikaku*)

What is common consciousness? Before I answer to this, let me try to talk a bit about consciousness.

Consciousness means to become aware of something by oneself. This, in turn, does not mean to discover something that others do not know, nor does it mean that one should not learn from others. To become aware of something by oneself refers to things, no matter whether learned from others or discovered by oneself, that one digests deeply in one's mind and makes one's own. Moreover, if we distinguish consciousness in terms of social class, we come up with several differences. The consciousness of a priest is not the same as that of a politician. The consciousness of a priest is also probably different from that of a philosopher. In fact, even priests, depending on their geographic location and historical period, cannot be said to all be the same.

Thus, there are myriad differences in consciousness, depending on the person, time, and place; however, there must be something that is common to them all. There must something that is at stake for all of them, as they all live in this world. The learned and the uneducated, the noble and the lowly, the rich and the poor—there is something they must become conscious of through cooperation. This is what I call "common consciousness."

Conscious Action

The development of an individual and the development of a nation can be considered to be the same process. For example, when an individual is still a child, all of its interests (*rigai*) depend exclusively on those of its father, elder brother, and the elders (*chōja*). But when one grows up, he will not follow blindly his father or elder brother against his own will; in other words, he will act in a conscious way. In the same fashion, when a nation is in its infancy, people are subjugated to other people: those of great strength, vast knowledge, and immense wealth. However, when members of a society advance to the point of acquiring consciousness of their ability to become free, all individuals begin to participate in politics, from the village on up to the state. At first, we the people are taught that our existence depends upon the sovereign, and we accept this idea blindly, but eventually we acquire consciousness that the government is an organism working for us, the people. People then become able to advocate democracy.

I don't know what the consciousness of a priest or a scholar is, but for those of us who are satisfied with the consciousness of common people (*heimin*), we think that it is enough if each individual among the people will acquire consciousness to this extent. Therefore, in the following chapters, I will discuss common people's consciousness.

1. Individual consciousness
2. Family consciousness
3. Factory consciousness
4. Municipality consciousness
5. National consciousness
6. World consciousness

Individual Consciousness

If we look at the long history of the human race, we find that in the beginning, humans lived contented with the fruits given to them by nature, or on fish, birds, and animals; to protect themselves from the weather, they could do nothing but take shelter under trees or in caves. They were in this condition for a long time. However, the human race has as its progenitor a mysterious holy spirit (*fukashigi no seirei*) that makes us progress without pause until we reach the ultimate. Our progress may be as slow as the steps of a cow, but we have passed down that immortal spirit to our sons and grandsons, and until now we have been struggling against the immense power of nature. Because of that struggle, today we have agriculture, animal husbandry, and industries that satisfy our desires for clothing, food, and dwelling; for our spiritual dimension, there are schools, churches, and books for the continuous improvement and progress of our spirit.

But our spirit is not satisfied with all this and, day and night, it continues fighting against our external circumstances. How long must we keep struggling before we can stop? There is no simple answer to that. However, there is something we do know. If we look at the traces left by our ancestors, and if we observe the spirit carried by the blood coursing through our arteries, there we hear the incessant sound "freedom, freedom." Yes, our ancestors, consciously or unconsciously, have been struggling for this freedom, and since we share the very same spirit, we too must keep on fighting until victory, no matter how strong nature's hardships and how cruel the rulers' despotism.

What is the freedom we will achieve after this struggle? To put it simply, it is being able to act always according to one's will, without ever being obstructed or bothered by anyone. That is, it means to always respect one's own will while at the same time respecting the will of the others, and to live in peace. In short, the final goal of the human race is independence and mutual aid, the realization of freedom, equality, and fraternity.[1] If we look at the evolution of politics, law, religion, and ethics, they have been developing from heteronomy toward autonomy; thus, after attaining self-governance the people will use their eventual individual surpluses to compensate for others' insufficiencies. This is natural evolution, and this is also the ultimate ideal of life. Everyone should fight and strive toward this goal.

Many seem to doubt that these ideas will improve the lot of all people. The doubters stress that human beings are just a kind of animal; their animal nature, which forces them to ignore others in order to satisfy their own desires, cannot be eliminated, as it is based in our bodies. However, as in the old verse, "take the weeds from the paddy field, and they will become fertilizer,"[2] with the development of the spirit, the effort toward satisfying one's endless desires will be perceived as inferior to enjoying life together with all others.

How do we know this? Because many of our ancestors have said so. As in the saying, "eliminate selfishness and act with benevolence (*onore wo koroshite jin wo nasu*),"[3] you all know many people who have saved their fellows from hardship even at the cost of their own precious lives. Besides, aren't there in the army today hundreds of thousands of young people in the prime of their youth from all over the country, ready to give their lives any time for their nation?

When we think about all these facts, we understand that we human beings are not like cows or horses; we are not made to live subjected to authoritarian rule but instead need to be independent and free to act as we choose. This is what we call the individual's common consciousness.

No matter how well government develops, no matter how kindly public officials lead us, they will never be able to satisfy our ideal. The more complicated the government becomes, the more corrupt it gets. Isn't it the same for tribunals? The criminal should repent autonomously and restrain himself. No matter how well the trial has been conducted, no one will know the truth better than the criminal. In particular, there is nothing more dangerous than to pass judgment on the basis of fragmentary proof. Today's government and legal system cannot function without ignoring human personality. This is part of the evolutionary process, and our consciousness must fight against it.

People commonly say that women differ from men, in that they don't need to be explicitly taught the art of living; for them, they say, it's enough to keep the house in order and raise their children. But the people who think this are very wrong. Especially today, with a huge gap between rich and poor due to the system of private ownership, this argument is profoundly mistaken. Women are not men's belongings. When husband and wife make a family together, the man is mainly responsible for securing the means of livelihood, whereas the woman, as his assistant, keeps order at home. This may be good as a method for division of labor; however, life is impermanent. The wife doesn't know when and for what reason she might be separated from her husband. When that happens, she, who until then had been making a living out of her husband's patrimony, should be able to live off her own work without any inconvenience. Today, many people, even women, work. Especially women who are left alone with small children, when the time comes to give the children an education, if the women have no job they find themselves in deep desperation. One could perhaps say that these women should remarry, but then the tragedy of life would only repeat itself.

Someone says that if we take ten people, all ten would disagree with what I just said. Indeed, that is true. One does not have to learn a profession just in anticipation of separation from one's husband. Since men and women are equal as individuals, they must work in order to raise their children and support their parents. Thus, women must also work. Theirs should not be a dependent and submissive work as befitting someone who belongs to a man; instead, women should learn an independent profession. There seem to be many contrary opinions to this. Old habits in particular will not make it easy to realize our ideas, but nonetheless we should make up our minds and strive to achieve them.

We human beings, firmly based on this consciousness, should reflect on our present condition. Then, in the same way as we don't regret giving up our life for the state, we should keep fighting for freedom.

We human beings are all different, and some of us will be far from attaining such consciousness; others will be closer to it. Others still, having overcome this common consciousness, might be waiting at a loftier dimension. In any case, everyone should advance to this stage. Even though you are like travelers at dusk at the foot of a mountain, you should not be discouraged, because you will certainly advance step by step toward the top of that mountain called consciousness. Isn't it so? Anyone who looks attentively at human history will understand that all people, the wise and the fool, and also the poor, are heading toward the shore of freedom, each in their own way.

Thus, from the standpoint of such consciousness, how shall each of us human beings act? First of all, the adults, men and women, who are able to leave their fathers and elder brothers and live independently should take care of their own lives autonomously. When one's individual desire clashes with someone else's, they should talk with each other and make efforts to accommodate one another. In other words, one should improve upon the habit of giving to others what one desires for oneself. Then, no matter how many social groups will have been formed, it will be possible to live in peace, each developing in full one's characteristics without hurting the others.

The family, the state, the entire world: they are all aggregations of individuals, and if each individual simply lived and acted according to pure-hearted kindness (*magokoro*)—that is, with a spirit of independence and freedom, the will to help the weak, and caring for one's neighbor—we would all be able to lead a peaceful and perfect collective life. We human beings should develop our spirit of independence and solidarity and fight against those who oppose this, even at the risk of our own lives.

Family Consciousness

The family is the social group closest to an individual, and if it were composed only of individuals who have acquired consciousness, it would be possible to get closer to freedom day by day, smoothly and without problems. However, the family is not composed only of individuals who have acquired consciousness. There may be a grandfather and grandmother who were born during the feudal age, there may be a wife who comes from a background with different habits from those of her husband's family, and there may be children born later. A family is a group composed of all these people. The head of the household, its center, must make a very strong effort to bring the light of freedom to all.

First of all, the head of the household who has acquired consciousness should act every day with the intention to teach the other family members—his parents, grandparents, sisters, and wife. The householder with a family of three or five should, as a matter of fact, always eat his three daily meals with his family; except when circumstances prevent him from doing so, he should avoid eating elsewhere. It won't be easy to do, but it is the duty of each single head of household to keep the good custom of taking meals together with his family. In addition, he should prepare soft food especially for the elders; everyone should put the elders first in accordance with the custom to treat elders with respect.

Even when there are guests, it is particularly important to have meals together with one's family. There may be cases in which this is inconvenient, and some people might think that this is a form of disrespect toward the guests. However, the householder who has acquired the consciousness that one should abandon self-conceit and share joys and sorrows with one's family, should act in this way and break old customs. In an ordinary family, difficulties arise from financial problems. In the case of a guest requiring the trouble of an extraordinary expenditure of 50 *sen*,[4] the householder who has attained consciousness should use those 50 *sen*, calmly and unashamedly, for a banquet for the whole family [and not only for the guest]. If you act in this way, you can easily imagine the happiness you will bring to your family life.

It goes without saying that the householder who has acquired consciousness should never ever make use of harmful food and drinks. Harmful substances are things such as sake and tobacco.

In addition to sharing food, clothing, and shelter impartially, and distributing chores among the family members according to their abilities, there should be a home economics meeting (*kaseikai*) once a week or once a month, where family concerns should be discussed among all family members under the coordination of the head of the family. In this way, regardless of [the family's] wealth or poverty, a family will be a little paradise.

Next, when children are born, from when they wear diapers they are raised by the mothers, but the head of the family who has acquired consciousness should not neglect his duties toward the children. As they say, "the soul of a three-year-old child attains one hundred years." Accordingly, one should not forget to infuse one's own spirit that has acquired consciousness from the time of a child's infancy. Toward that goal, while taking good care to protect the child, one should try to raise the child in the habit to acting as much as possible in its own way. Concerning children's education and choice of profession, parents should advise them upon considering their qualities, but should never force something upon them. When the time comes for one's son to choose a wife, also in this case parents should respect his freedom; they should instruct him to fight against freedom's enemies.

The greatest troubles for a family come not from wife, siblings, or children, but from one's parents and grandparents, who are from a different era. It is not easy to influence people who hold on to a fixed way of thinking and who have kept old customs for many years. The head of the household should help them acquire consciousness by holding formal conversations with them during family gatherings at least once a week. Since truth will eventually triumph one day, the light of freedom will doubtlessly and without fail illuminate the whole family and bestow its blessings upon all.

Villagers' Consciousness

Villages, towns, and cities are the smallest organizations among local governments. In particular, the inhabitants of towns rather than cities, and those of villages rather than towns [have had close] human relations since the time of their ancestors, and these are the most intimate communities after the family. There are even villages composed of one extended family; if we look at their ancestors we find out that many of them come from either the same family or are related to one single family. Since a village is an extended family, one should expect to find in it no large differences of rank and wealth as appropriate to the most harmonious paradise of peace; however, present conditions prevent it from being so.

The cause for that is vainglory, promoted as the most important aspect of our society; this consists in ignoring the others and trying to be successful alone. Another cause, I believe, is the enormous influence of the system of private property.

In the distant past, land, the most important asset in a village, was all held in common. With population growth, since land does not increase, the system of private property was introduced. At the beginning, each individual was allotted the same amount of land, but since human life keeps changing year after year, generation after generation, natural disasters and individual predispositions over a long time resulted sometimes in family dispersion. Then, some people took advantage of other people's misfortune and tried to satisfy their own desire. This is how differences in wealth originated, even in a village in which at the beginning everyone was equal; this situation still continues today.

Since material conditions (food, clothing, and shelter) have a great influence in human life, the gap separating the rich and the poor, which is largely related to such material conditions, necessarily affects the constitution and character of each individual. Even in minor things, the rich call the poor filthy and vulgar: just talking with them is polluting. The poor, on their part, point to the pompous manners of the rich and slander them behind their backs by saying that the rich are full of hot air and are unable to produce even one single grain of rice, that money doesn't last forever, and that they cannot do how they please all the time just because they have money.

Even under today's system of local autonomy, in the same village there are those who enjoy civil rights and those who don't. Those with civil rights can participate in the administration of the village, but those without them are not allowed such participation. Even among those who enjoy civil rights, there are distinctions in the rights to which they are entitled, as in the electorate of first and second class (*ikkyū senmin, nikyū senmin*).[5] In short, even in local administration, there are three kinds of differences among the people of the same village. In addition, we cannot fathom the damages inflicted on the personality of schoolchildren because of differences in wealth; the same is also true about participation in village rituals.

In other words, you would expect that, as inhabitants of the same village, people would have mutual interactions of the most intimate and peaceful nature, but that is not the case, primarily because of the distinction between the rich and the poor; and what makes such distinction even more important is the system of private property.

How can we redress this situation? To put it bluntly, since it would be difficult to abolish the present system of private property and replace it with collectivization, we should at first urge the persons of influence to build many public facilities and let all villagers enjoy them.

The mayor who governs the village should certainly increase the collective resources and actively establish institutions of compulsory education such as elementary schools, in order to promote [among villagers] knowledge [useful] to increase the village's economic production. He should also establish municipal and trade-union hospitals, public hygiene facilities not only limited to [treatment of] contagious diseases, that are free for patients from the village. Next, he should establish a town hall at the center of the village, where ceremonies (*kankon sōsai*) can be performed, where the residents of the village can have friendly exchanges: meetings of senior citizens, young people, married women, young girls etc. Expenses for these activities should all be drawn from public funds, so as to make participation in these gatherings possible irrespective of individual wealth.

It goes without saying that the prohibition against harmful drinks and food should be upheld in the same way as in families who have acquired consciousness. No matter how well organized the village government, if it allows harmful habits such as sake, tobacco, and gambling, it risks spoiling everything despite having put so much effort into this.

Municipal Consciousness

Residents of cities, towns, and villages should acquire essentially the same consciousness, but since there are great differences in wealth and status, the leaders should have the highest consciousness and make the strongest effort, otherwise it will be difficult to attain the level of consciousness necessary in cities and towns. To that purpose, the mayors and the members of municipal assemblies should exercise the spirit of public interest, respect the individuality of each resident, and establish adequate public facilities. They should be especially generous with the creation of professional schools that form the basis of independent economic activity for men and women. They should strive to increase the fundamental assets (common wealth) of urban residents so that they can enjoy a peaceful life and develop refined tastes.

Factory Consciousness[6]

What is the industrial sector? Before I talk about this, it is perhaps necessary to outline the development of industry. Early modern industrial development began in an age in which industry was a family economic activity, and then shifted to the age of handicraft. Later it further evolved into the present age of corporate industry.

It is possible to distinguish two kinds of corporate industry. The first is house industry; the second is factory industry. Now, is all industry part of corporate industry? Not necessarily. If we fill a box with soybeans, we cannot add more soybeans to it, but there is still some room for millet or sesame; in the same way, even though great corporate industry is becoming prominent, family industry and handicraft still exist. In general, all everyday commodities such as food, shelter, and clothing—commodities necessary to human life—in particular have come to be produced by large factories because of what we could consider, from the point of view of economic evolution, a natural law. Therefore, we should understand that what we call industry consciousness only refers to large factories.

A society that has acquired consciousness needs to be ordered in a well-regulated fashion, and the method to realize this consists first in hygiene, second, in convenience (*benri*), and third, in ornaments, all of which should be evenly universalized. Since the industry sector supplies commodities needed by society, industry should be organized according to the same method.

First, it is obvious that each local area should operate its characteristic and most convenient industries according to general estimates of supply and demand in the entire world, but it is natural that manufacturing should be carried out as close as possible to the place of production of the raw materials. Today's industrial sector is based on a nation's economy, and the state aims for self-sufficiency; to that purpose, it enforces protectionist and tariff policies and engages in international competition. As I see it, this is a ridiculous policy, and even though it might be unavoidable as a step in the process toward the acquisition of consciousness, I believe that this useless and harmful international competition should be abolished immediately. These policies cause immeasurable damage to our project to build a paradise.

The first measure that is necessary to carry out this program is to establish a worldwide labor union for each factory in the same sector (cotton mills, textile factories, etc.); after estimating the demand for the year, production will be distributed to each factory, which will have to provide [its share of the] supply. Today's system of private property's exclusive focus on personal interest is a problem, but the entire industrial world ends up pursuing only this.

An opponent might say that this would create a huge monopoly that would control the means of production, with the result that the buyer would be charged unfairly high prices. Certainly, from the perspective of the present system, this is perhaps not an unreasonable concern. This is why we emphasize shared ownership of the means of production. Aside from art and luxury items, necessary commodities such as clothing, food, and shelter, which are indispensable to everyone, should all be supplied by communal factories. This is the bottom line.

This is the level of consciousness that we have to attain and we should act with this as our compass. Those who try to stop us should be wiped away.

As for the method itself, it is conceivable that both capitalists and workers who have acquired consciousness will find the necessary clues and start the whole process.

The capitalist who has acquired consciousness will reject the old crime of living out of his capital and will come to realize that all human beings must secure their clothing and food through their own labor—this is what the old sages called paradise (*tengoku*) or the land of the gods (*shinkoku*). After making his own capital available without compensation to all as a resource for livelihood, he will think of how best to employ his talent and labor in order to realize such a paradise as soon as possible.

What should the workers who have acquired consciousness do? Each of them should master a technique they like and, in accordance with their natural disposition, they should strive to make the despotic capitalists feel remorse and amend their ways. In order to do so, they should strengthen the unity of the workers. Each [worker] should make contributions, and require the capitalists to also make contributions, [to a common relief fund] in order to neutralize as much as possible the effects of both natural and human-caused disasters.

They should establish collective scholastic institutions so that the children of the workers can more easily receive an education. Moreover, a method of insurance should be devised in order to protect the elderly and those affected by incurable diseases; collective hospitals should be established and made accessible to all in cases of emergency. Collective clubs (recreational organizations) should be established so that the tastes and the knowledge [of the workers] can be improved and developed. Furthermore, factories should turn into collective properties of all the workers, thereby realizing democracy in the industrial sector; this is the first step toward the realization of paradise.

I'm just listing these things, but the path leading us there has mountains and valleys, and they will not let us walk through it easily. Many comrades will have to shed their blood along the way. The workers who have acquired consciousness should take the lead and try out this process in advance.

Those who spend their lives, no matter how long, without acquiring consciousness, and those who have acquired consciousness but just follow their whims without [putting their consciousness into] action, are destined to enter into annihilation (*horobi ni iru*); those who act in accordance with their consciousness, even if they should die when they are just seven years old, will achieve eternal life (*eisei*). The saying by Confucius, "if one has heard the Way in the morning, it is all right to die in the evening,"[7] refers to what I just said, because that person has been involved, even just a little, in the realization of paradise. Conscious action also involves many painful experiences, such as separation from one's parents, abandoning one's wife and children, being misunderstood by one's friends. However, the fall of one individual is for the happiness of many in society; as the saying goes, "except a corn of wheat fall into the ground and die, it abideth alone; but if it die, it bringeth forth much fruit."[8] In this way, by overcoming many difficulties in order to put one's consciousness into practice, one will repeatedly bask in one's holy spirit as a conscious person and will be able to engage in self-cultivation in everyday life.

Such a wholesome worker, ready to die in the struggle for paradise, is the person most loved by god. Because of that, even the most stubborn capitalists and the classes in power will be able to acquire consciousness of their sins. It's up to the worker who has acquired consciousness to put all his or her effort into this.

Agricultural Consciousness

Considering the fact that agriculture originated before industry, it would seem that agricultural consciousness should be achieved sooner than that of industry, but in fact this is not the case, and industry appears to be attaining consciousness ahead of agriculture. This is due to the fact that the industrial workers come from an agricultural background. Their motivation for becoming industrial workers is that arable land, which is the foundation of production, is limited, but the reproduction of the human population is limitless, so the population in excess tends to move to the cities and become industrial workers. Moreover, during the feudal period, when there was no freedom to migrate like today, many second and third sons of farmers were not able to establish their own independent family but lived all their lives with their parents or elder brothers (*heyazumi*). Because of these circumstances, those who move away are persons of initiative, whereas those who remain in their villages and continue their forefathers' activities are conservative; therefore, they are in general slower to acquire consciousness.

However, as the sprouts of the new grass emerge underneath the snow in the spring, even though the snow has not completely melted in the valleys, so, following the acquisition of consciousness in the industrial sector, the agricultural sector will also acquire consciousness.

The acquisition of agricultural consciousness should also begin with common ownership of the land. This will follow the acquisition of consciousness by both landowners and tenant farmers; the landowners, in particular, should study this in depth. No one doubts that the land originally exists in nature; there are several legal arguments about its becoming private property in the present time. If we consider the facts, however, our distant ancestors originally developed the land and, as a result of their long labor, it has become today's cultivable land. Accordingly, we can only conclude that, as a matter of principle, today's landowners' exclusive property of the land and their request of half of the harvest are great crimes.

Even though opponents argue that the present landowners have bought their land at considerable expense and therefore haven't committed any wrong, purchasing the land was itself wrong. If we think that this was a lawful action, then buying and selling stolen property should also be considered lawful. Furthermore, the very money used for that purchase is the accumulation of labor, and much capital originates from stealing the accumulation of honest labor. In other words, it is like power squeezing the blood out of the weak. If landowners wish to enter the realm of consciousness and bask in the happiness of eternal life, they should not try these twisted arguments.

To put it bluntly, everyone should make a living through one's work. Private property of the land and acquisition of clothing and food through stealing others' labor leads to eternal extinction. Acquiring consciousness of this situation, one should turn the land into common property and, accordingly, all workers should be entitled to the harvest of their own work. Each worker should acquire clothing and food according to their talent and effort, and live peacefully in this paradise of happiness.

Next, the agricultural workers, in view of the above truth, should make the landowners look into their own conscience, and for that purpose, the method should be. . . .

Fragment from a Prison Manuscript
(*Gokuchū shuki*)

. . . it's a . . . system; it's despotic.

As for myself, if I have to choose between two possibilities, namely, whether to die without any of the good or bad things I previously discussed, or to die after having lived "thick and short," like, if I can't leave behind a good name, at least I should leave a bad one, I don't subscribe to either choice, but at least I hope that, for the happiness of those people, clinging to my solid and unmovable beliefs, I can endeavor so that they may act freely.

I wish that they will act according to the demands of reason/principle and not out of material desires based on physical urges, or on the basis of impulsive emotions. If their action is in accordance with the demands of reason, even if the plan fails halfway through and one vanishes like dew on the scaffold, one will still be able to smile in detachment, but otherwise, if one has acted because of an impulsive emotion, when things go well the result will be the same, but in misfortune one will not be able to avoid begrudging people and crying bitterly at heaven because of one's pain; in that case, I feel sorry for them.

What does it mean to act according to reason? Some people say that such a thing is easy for the intellectuals but we cannot really expect it from ordinary people. Perhaps it is so. However, I believe that there are many differences in how one acts according to reason: university people as university people, middle school pupils as middle school pupils; thus, uneducated commoners can also act according to reason without regret. Below, I would like to talk about this.

What is reason? Or rather, instead of talking about such a stiff and difficult thing, [let me ask] something more at hand, namely, how does the human race progress? Let's examine this quickly.

First, from the perspective of hygiene [that is, the material conditions of life,], wouldn't we all like to be able to consume as much as needed of the three elements of clothing, food, and shelter? With that, I don't mean things such as being able to live in a high marble mansion, or to wear a kimono sash worth one thousand yen, or even to eat at a banquet worth a hundred yen per person. No, we don't want such luxuries.

What we are looking for is to work for about ten hours every day, to have about one day of vacation once a week; to wear appropriate clothes in the cold and hot seasons; to be given enough nourishment when one is sick; to have the possibility to enjoy, to a certain degree, art and entertainment, and to carry out religious pursuits of one's choice during the holidays. Isn't this what we all would like to do? This is not just my own desire, but everyone's desire. This is the extent of the ideals we pursue; it is one's duty to advance toward these goals even with one leg.

In order to achieve this goal, it is necessary to examine the present situation of society and one's condition within it. How is society today? While there are people who build palaces worth three hundred yen a *tsubo*[9] on a plot of land worth one hundred yen a *tsubo*, aren't there also shopkeepers paying three yen per month for a six-*tatami* room, families of six who live in one room in a row house, and workers who can barely survive? In fact, there are even people who cannot afford a place to live and have to find rest from the day's fatigue under an eave on a street in the cold winter sky, with the stars as their companions. This is our society. Today, there are people who can afford to wear clothes worth one or two thousand yen apiece, and people who, even in winter, must wear only one workman's short coat (*hanten*), and their children must also wear dirty rags. This is the condition of the workers today.

Compulsory education now lasts six years. We should be merely thankful for this true blessing of an enlightened age, but unfortunately for ordinary workers this is a painful and bitter matter. The children of ordinary workers are born under the miserable condition that, at nine or ten years old, they must work somehow in order to help their parents. When their parents compare their situation to that of the rich kids, with their privilege to have their military service delayed so that they can keep going to school until they are twenty-five or thirty, will not their hearts be justly upset?

The gentlemen eat cuisine that costs five or even ten yen per meal and then feel weak because it's difficult to digest, whereas the workers have difficulty affording a five-cent lunch box; what star is responsible for this fate? There is a worker whose father is more than sixty years old and has been lying in bed sick for two months now. Not only can he not see a doctor, he cannot even afford to buy medicine, even though there are many doctors and medical students in the universities. Many excellent hospitals are built, but aren't they beyond the reach of workers?

Now, in such a society, to see people who give up, saying "that's [just] the way things are" and who live like pigs in a barn, sustaining themselves day by day with other people's leftovers, and living worse than the dogs of the millionaires; or who spend all their life as menial workers, forced to live alone without a family and with just one short coat for the whole year. A talented youth arouses one's manly vigor and throws away half of his life to investigate the causes of this injustice in order to reform this unjust society. A man of firm character absorbs the theories about social happiness formulated by scholars throughout the world's history and starts an action movement, but unfortunately in the midst of his activity has to bear the suffering of prison. A man like Sakura Sōgorō, who was crucified for having appealed directly to the authorities in order to alleviate the hardships of many peasants; or people like Ōshio Heihachirō, who, during a famine without precedent in history, angered by the [local] magistrate's lack of humaneness, attacked the rice warehouses of Tenma in Osaka in an unsuccessful attempt to alleviate the hunger of many poor people. Those who have acted according to their firm beliefs must be considered happiest among human beings.

A religious man like Śākyamuni gave up the throne and became a mendicant; a philosopher like Diogenes spent his entire life in a tub. Both lived lives full of joy and gratification that couldn't be taken away from them even by the emperor. Jesus Christ was killed on the cross, but nonetheless, claiming that by doing so he was compensating for everyone's sins, he rejoiced in death. People who have acted according to their principles are happy people. Thus, participating as much as one can in various movements with the goal, as all people equally desire, that everyone in this society can work in just conditions and receive fair supplies of clothing, food, and shelter—isn't this a form of acting according to one's principles? One can live as calmly as they do normal conditions even though, just because one has acted according to one's principle, one will become like dew on the scaffold or be insulted on the cross, or again finish his life in a subterranean prison in Hokkaido with the cold winter wind piercing one's bones;[10] this is what is called happiness in life.

What, then, is the method to achieve this?

December 26, 1909
Gudō

Appendix

Original Works Published
by Uchiyama Gudō

English Translation of
"Aux conscripts"

(from *L'anarchie*)

Comrades,

In a few days, the most beautiful and sweet among the Fatherlands is going to order some of you to abandon your family home, to separate yourselves from the tender affections of your father, your mother, your lover, and your friends, to go through a two-year encampment with the army.

This is after you have been prepared by the school and the family to the idea of Fatherland; it is after you have been taught to consider an enemy each human being with different customs and language and living outside conventional limits called borders, that they, under the pretext of national defense and under the name of achieved freedoms, impose upon you a degrading slavery.

However, if the defense of France is the principal cause for this imposition, why aren't the troops that form the army spread along the borders and coasts? What are they doing in the interior of the nation?

All regimes, all governments that have succeeded themselves have always employed this force for what they have agreed to call keeping the internal order, which means, in clear and precise terms, the defense of the coffer and the protection of the classes of speculators against the logical claims of the proletariat.

Hasn't a bourgeois economist, J. B. Say, said that "Far from protecting national independence, a large military establishment is perhaps that which endangers it most, because of the aggressive tendencies which it provokes among those who can use it." Oh, yes! These old words still deserve to be pondered today.

Indeed, what are they going to order you [to do], after making you wear that ridiculous uniform?

To ignore your individuality, to compress any initiative and all intellectual life, and to subject yourselves to a degrading obedience submitted to an idiotic hierarchy which is the negation of all reasoning. They will tell you that the orders from your superiors must be carried out without murmur, without critical examination, with blind faith.

In addition to the hatred for foreigners, which you have already acquired, they will teach [you] to consider as equally contemptible those who, even though they are born in your same land, have a conception against passive obedience or acceptance of rules imposed by the government.

And when they will have destroyed completely your critical spirit and sense of freedom, you will become killing machines that they will use to establish the reign of arbitrariness upon ignorance.

You will also be employed in a humiliating police service of provocation in order to perpetuate serfdom for the industry bosses and poverty, and tomorrow you will share in this serfdom as your life's lot. You, sons of workers, will put your energy to the service of our oppressors, in order to reduce all impulse of generous revolt of the oppressed. It will be you who, frightened by fear of punishment, upon a barbaric order from your superiors, shoot loosely at your fathers, your mothers, your brothers, your sisters, your friends: because you will end up killing indiscriminately the parents of those who will execute the same orders in your hometowns.

It is in order to combat such egoistic fanaticism of Fatherland and Army in all its forms—as it destroys in the individual the revolutionary spirit of human solidarity—that we tell you, young people, to whom habits are always more important than reason, that it is time to reject all these religious and secular metaphysics, which are only useful to consolidate the privilege of a few while preserving the bad conditions and misery of the vast majority.

Glory, honor, the army, fatherland, god—all vague terms which, nevertheless, have become magical, and with which past and present rulers have kept and still keep the masses under their yoke.

All wars are criminal endeavors; they are only for the advantage of the plutocracy that governs us and the stockjobbers who exploit us! That's why we tell you: stop being sacrificial lambs, throw anathema upon the murderers, stop being remissive slaves; turn into thinking beings, resolved to defend not the interests of your masters but your own rights to life.

The Fatherland is sweet to the rich, inexorable to the unfortunate. The Fatherland perpetuates the antagonism and continues the most rabid authoritarianism.

It is in order to maintain such tyrannical state that you are going to sacrifice two good years of your youth and perhaps your life.

If your thoughtlessness takes you to a strike, you may be sure that the brutal actions of your spineless service of the defense of capital by oppressing your brothers will turn against you. On the other hand, aren't you going to be tomorrow's oppressed?

When they send you to the border or on a colonial expedition, you will again sacrifice your lives just for some maggoty banker or shameless speculator, and if you then return home, sick and miserable, what is your Mother Country going to do for you? Nothing.

This Mother is none other than an [evil] stepmother!

That is why we antimilitarists have decided to respond to all war declarations with insurrection.

Do not think that we reject one master just to accept the oppression of another soldier with spurs and crown . . . especially as the antimilitarist activity we do here is also done, with more intensity, elsewhere.

To fight the armies means to open up a new age to the science of happiness.

Break up the circle of obsolete traditions, so that the blindfold they have wanted you to keep over your eyes no longer hides the sun. Slaves, break your chains, so that your brains can become lovers of beautiful revolutionary disobedience, and if your blood must flow, may it be for your Happiness and your Freedom.

"Anti-Moral Considerations"

by Max Baginski

The rulers and possessors also have hard problems to solve. How shall they fortify their threatened privileges? How to strengthen the weakening faith of the people in the "justice" of the State; how to lull their ever-growing suspicion as to the corruption of wealth and power?

The faith and respect of the masses are indispensable to the rulers; without them no government is safe. They must therefore be artificially inculcated by the aid of the family, the church, the school, patriotic phrases, and the habits of mental indolence.

Formerly this was a much less difficult problem. The invention of printing, however, in spite of the wholesale spreading of prejudice and lies, was instrumental in aiding some revolutionizing ideas to gain currency—brave, noble thoughts disturbed the lethargy of the people and made them think. And with thought came doubt and the question: Are the "accepted truths" really true? Is current, official justice really just?

Ah, the good old days when priest and ruler could read the destinies of nations in the flight of birds and the intestines of cattle! In those times the people had more confidence in the oracles than they have nowadays in the integrity of legislatures, whose corruption is becoming daily more apparent.

The long entertained suspicion is gradually crystallizing into the firm conviction that our political, religious, and social institutions are but the reins with which the producing masses are kept "in order," to be exploited and oppressed at the will of their rulers.

This realization is fatal for the upper four hundred—they must look around for new ways and means to continue their slaves in subjection.

The power of religion is not nearly as effective as before. True, many thousands of churches are still making the earth hideous, like the telltale marks of a smallpox victim. 'Tis a land of religion and puritanism: the law-givers begin their work with prayers. But so do also certain Italian banditti, who consecrate wax candles to Sancta Maria in the pious hope that their next robber excursion will prove the more successful.

In reality, however, religion has lost its influence upon our social and economic actions. It lacks the power to help the "good" and defeat the "evil." The good God is treated like some business partner who is often taken advantage of and cheated.

This form of piousness Clarence Darrow has fittingly characterized at Boise: "You may kill, steal, commit any crime known to heaven or to earth, and then you may turn and throw your crime on somebody else and your soul upon God."

Indeed, religion does not prevent the rich from robbing and oppressing the poor. On the other hand, however, it has fortunately ceased to serve as a barrier for the masses in the expression of their social and economic aspirations and demands.

Religion is thus ineffectual in conserving the masses in bondage. A substitute has become necessary. It is urgently demanded and found in—morality.

The moral precepts, like the religious, are authoritarian in character. True, 'tis not the old God that issues the commands. His place has been taken by the "moral conscience," "duty," "the inner voice"; the tyranny, before external, has now become internal. The religious fetters of faith in divine and earthly authority are growing weaker and threaten to break: morality must come to the rescue, that the aspirations of humanity, the cry of the masses for life and joy, be stifled in its iron grip.

Education and literature are eternally multiplying the number of our "duties" and the demands made upon us. Every sign of awakening of the growing—or already grown—individual is eradicated by a moral command. Our moral guardians are no less tyrannical and intolerant than those of law and religion. They even dare to prescribe moral precepts for science, philosophy, and art.

Having put under its ban the free association of the sexes, morality has succeeded in fostering forced marriage, prostitution, and venereal diseases. Men and women must not satisfy their physiological needs, except [if] they are married; but as economic misery prevents marriage in a great many cases—and that at the very period when sex life is most imperative—nothing remains for them but celibacy or prostitution. Such are the blessings of our economics and morality.

Anarchism, negating compulsion in all phases of human activity, political, economic and social, is consequently also antagonistic to all commands of morality, which is but the masked instrument of subjection.

During the recent strike of the drivers of the New York Street Cleaning Department, the press and authorities denounced the strikers because they neglected their "duty," their "moral obligation" toward the city and the public.

An excellent example of bourgeois morality! Is it the duty of under-paid and ill-treated employees to keep the city's streets clean—especial-ly the quarters of the rich? The same duty commands them to patiently suffer the filth of their misery and rot in their economic swamp, that the rich may continue their life of parasitic idleness. In truth, morality is a well-paying business—for the rich, the exploiters. But the poor were doomed to eternal servitude were it not for the happy circumstance that they prefer to be immoral.

In the same sense, people prate of "moral satisfaction" in work well done. Are we not all familiar with the phrase, "the dignity of labor"? The hypocrites! The man of spirit and independence can but feel hu-miliated by his forced labor; far from enjoying "moral satisfaction" in his wage slavery, he can not help but be filled with hatred against con-ditions which degrade him to a mere tool for the accumulation of wealth—for others. The proletarian whose spirit does not rise in protest against his degrading bondage is a born slave, lacking all manhood.

Morality condemns encroachments upon property. It is the "moral duty" of the homeless one to pass quietly by the mansion of the mil-lionaire. Were he to enter, to rest up his weary body, he would be brand-ed a criminal, fit for prison. Morality is thus anti-social and unnatural. Morality shouts, "Stop thief!" when a hungry tramp has taken a loaf of bread, and then proceeds to bow before and worship the successful em-ployer who daily robs his workingmen of half the value of their product.

Morality is a practiced hypocrite, whom no free spirit may welcome.

Notes

Preface

1 Riccardo Pedrini, *Libera Baku ora* (Rome: DeriveApprodi, 2000).

2 See Hans Magnus Enzesberger, *La breve estate dell'anarchia: vita e morte di Buenaventura Durruti* (Milan: Feltrinelli, 1973).

3 See, for instance, Kashiwagi Ryūhō, ed., *Taigyaku jiken no shūhen: Heiminsha chihō dōshi no hitobito* (Tokyo: Ronsōsha, 1980).

4 A view on the global scope of anarchism at Gudō's time is provided by Alex Butterworth, *The World That Never Was: A True Story of Dreamers, Schemers, Anarchists & Secret Agents* (New York: Pantheon Books, 2010) and Benedict R. Anderson, *Under Three Flags: Anarchism and the Anti-colonial Imagination* (London and New York: Verso, 2005).

5 Meetings to achieve unanimity are still part of the anarchist tradition, including the recent popular movement Occupy Wall Street. A member of a Milanese anarchist commune in Italy says: "It is best not to vote when we have to take a decision all together. We discuss for hours until either we all agree or we decide not to do it; this is true 'democracy,' but this is also anarchism—no majority, no minority, no unhappy or undecided people" (quoted in the Italian newsmagazine *L'Espresso*, July 19, 2012, p. 85).

6 On a personal note, as someone who has lived and worked in Japan for many years, the amount of time spent by the average Japanese person in meetings of all kinds is staggering. Many meetings are not brainstorming sessions to produce new ideas but exercises in conformism; consensus-building is a form of indoctrination, much like the awareness-producing meetings Gudō envisioned. In this sense, at least, Gudō was less revolutionary and more in line with traditional Japanese mores than might usually be thought.

7 For an attempt at resituating the anarchist tradition in the contemporary cultural and political context, see Nathan J. Jun, *Anarchism and Political Modernity* (London and New York: Continuum, 2012).

8 See Rambelli, "Buddhist Republican Thought and Institutions in Japan: Preliminary Considerations," in *Japanese Studies Around the World 2008*, Special Issue "Scholars of Buddhism in Japan: Buddhist Studies in the 21st Century" (Kyoto: International Research Center for Japanese Studies, 2009, pp. 127–153.

9 On these issues, see the texts listed in n. 90.

10 For a preliminary overview, see Jean Chesneaux, "Egalitarian and Utopian Traditions in the East," *Diogenes* 16 (62) (1968): 76–102.

Introduction

1 For more on Engaged Buddhism, see Christopher S. Queen and Sallie B. King, eds., *Engaged Buddhism: Buddhist Liberation Movements in Asia* (Albany, NY: SUNY Press, 1996); Christopher S. Queen, ed., *Engaged Buddhism in the West* (Boston: Wisdom Publications, 2000); Sallie B. King, *Being Benevolence: The Social Ethics of Engaged Buddhism* (Honolulu: University of Hawai'i Press, 2005); Sallie B. King, *Socially Engaged Buddhism* (Honolulu: University of Hawai'i Press, 2009).

2 Dalai Lama, *Ethics for the New Millennium* (New York: Riverhead Books, 1999), pp. 175–176.

3 A. T. Ariyaratne, interviewed by Catherine Ingram in Catherine Ingram, *In the Footsteps of Gandhi: Conversations with Spiritual Social Activists* (Berkeley: Parallax Press, 1990), p. 133.

4 Thich Nhat Hanh, *Being Peace* (Berkeley: Parallax Press, 1987), p. 92.

5 Sulak Sivaraksa, "Buddhism and Human Rights in Siam," in Sulak Sivaraksa, ed., *Socially Engaged Buddhism for the New Millennium; Essays in Honor of the Ven. Phra Dhammapitaka (Bhikkhu P. A. Payutto) on His 60th Birthday Anniversary,* (Bangkok: Sathirakoses-Nagapradipa Foundation and Foundation for Children, 1999), p. 198.

6 Sivaraksa, "Buddhism and Human Rights in Siam," p. 199.

7 This account is largely drawn from Santikaro Bhikkhu, "Buddhadasa Bhikkhu: Life and Society Through the Natural Eyes of Voidness," in Queen and King, eds., *Engaged Buddhism: Buddhist Liberation Movements in Asia*, pp. 147–193.

8 This formula appears in several places in the Buddha's teachings; this citation is from the *Majjhima-Nikāya* 115, *Bahudhātuka Sutta*, translated by Bhikkhu Ñaṇamoli and Bhikkhu Bodhi, *The Middle Length Discourses of the Buddha: A New Translation of the Majjhima Nikāya* (Boston: Wisdom Publications, 1995), p. 927.

9 Santikaro Bhikkhu, quoting Buddhadasa Bhikkhu, in Queen and King, eds., *Engaged Buddhism: Buddhist Liberation Movements in Asia,* p. 166.

10 Santikaro Bhikkhu, quoting Buddhadasa Bhikkhu, in Queen and King, eds., *Engaged Buddhism: Buddhist Liberation Movements in Asia,* p. 167.

11 Dalai Lama, *Freedom in Exile: The Autobiography of the Dalai Lama* (New York: HarperCollins, 1990), pp. 268–269.

12 His Holiness: The XIV Dalai Lama of Tibet, "Human Rights and Universal Responsibility," in Damien V. Keown, Charles S. Prebish, and Wayne R. Husted,

eds., *Buddhism and Human Rights* (Richmond, UK: Curzon Press, 1998), p. xviii.

[13] Saneh Chamarik, "Buddhism and Human Rights," paper no. 12 (Bangkok: Thai Khadi Research Institute, Thammasat University, 1982), p. 5.

[14] Phra Rajavaramuni (P. A. Payutto), "Preamble," in Saneh Chamarik, "Buddhism and Human Rights," paper no. 12 (Bangkok: Thai Khadi Research Institute, Thammasat University, 1982), np.

Chapter 1

[1] Yoshida Kyūichi, *Nihon kindai bukkyōshi kenkyū*, in *Yoshida Kyūichi chosakushū* (Tokyo: Kawashima shoten, 1992), vol. 1, p. 403.

[2] Gudō only attended public elementary school; his middle-school education was part of his training as a Zen monk.

[3] At about the time when Gudō was resident priest, among the villagers of Ōhiradai 78 percent had an income of less than a hundred yen per year, whereas Watanabe made more than three thousand yen; see Kashiwagi Ryūhō, *Taigyaku jiken to Uchiyama Gudō* (Tokyo: JCA shuppan, 1979), p. 20.

[4] Morinaga Eizaburō, *Uchiyama Gudō* (Tokyo: Ronsōsha, 1984), pp. 65, 68.

[5] Kanzaki Kiyoshi, *Taigyaku jiken soshō kiroku, shōko bussha* (Tokyo: Kindai Nihon shiryō kenkyūkai, 1960–1962), vol. 8, p. 175.

[6] Concerning *ansatsushugi* (terrorism), in 1907 Japanese radical socialists published in the United States a bilingual leaflet, *"Ansatsushugi"*—"The Terrorism," which incited the murder of the emperor of Japan (John Crump, *The Origins of Socialist Thought in Japan* [London: Croom Helm; New York: St. Martin's Press, 1983], pp. 204–205). It is not clear, however, whether Gudō actually read this pamphlet (Kanzaki, *Taigyaku jiken soshō kiroku, shōko bussha*, vol. 2, p. 36).

[7] See F. G. Notehelfer, *Kōtoku Shūsui: Portrait of a Japanese Radical* (London: Cambridge University Press, 1971), pp. 109–132. Kōtoku explained his shift away from parliamentary politics toward direct action in the article "Yoga shisō no henka," published in *Heimin shinbun*, no. 16 (February 2, 1907), p. 1. See Asukai Masamichi, ed., *Kōtoku Shūsui shū* (Tokyo: Chikuma shobō, 1975), pp. 291–296; English translation in Crump, *The Origin of Socialist Thought in Japan*, pp. 341–350.

[8] Notehelfer, *Kōtoku Shūsui: Portrait of a Japanese Radical.*

[9] Morinaga, *Uchiyama Gudō*, pp. 121–122.

[10] Kanzaki, *Taigyaku jiken soshō kiroku, shōko bussha*, vol. 8, p. 176.

[11] The summary of the evidence against Gudō at the trial is presented in *Shakaishugi enkaku* (Tokyo: Misuzu shobō, 1982), vol. 1, pp. 70–71. The dynamite found at his temple seems to have been deposited there during the construction work for a dam in the nearby mountains; see Kanzaki, *Taigyaku jiken*

soshō kiroku, shōko bussha, vol. 8, p. 183. One portion of the complete court documents for the High Treason trial can be found in Kanzaki, *Taigyaku jiken soshō kiroku, shōko bussha;* a selection (which, however, includes only very few references to Uchiyama Gudō) is presented in Shioda Shōhei and Watanabe Junzō, eds., *Hiroku Taigyaku jiken,* 2 vols. (Tokyo: Shunjūsha, 1959). Kanzaki also published a general account of the incident, based on court records, *Kakumei densetsu taigyaku jiken,* 4 vols. (Tokyo: Kodomo no miraisha, 2010). Recently, the High Treason trial has been the subject of a novel by Saki Ryūzō, *Shōsetsu Taigyaku Jiken* (Tokyo: Bungei shunjū, 2001; Gudō is treated mostly on pp. 277–286); and a *manga* book by Natsuo Sekigawa and Jirō Taniguchi, *Au temps de Botchan,* 5 vols. (Paris: Seuil, 2005); Gudō appears in vol. 4, p. 213, and his work is discussed on pp. 233–235. On the impact of the High Treason Trial on modern Japanese literature, see Suga Hidemi, *"Teikoku" no bungaku: sensō to "Taigyaku" no aida* (Tokyo: Ibunsha, 2001). Tanaka Nobumasa, in *Taigyaku jiken: Shi to sei no gunzō* (Tokyo: Iwanami shoten, 2010), discusses the survivors of the trial and contemporary attempts to redress its verdict.

[12] Kanzaki, *Taigyaku jiken soshō kiroku, shōko bussha,* vol. 4, p. 218. Reported, in slightly different versions, by Yoshida, *Nihon kindai bukkyōshi kenkyū,* vol. 1, p. 436; and Morinaga, *Uchiyama Gudō,* p. 7.

[13] Gudō's official biography as it appears in the records of the Sōtō sect at around the time of the trial is published in Morinaga, *Uchiyama Gudō,* pp. 44–45.

[14] See Brian Victoria, *Zen at War* (New York and Tokyo: Weatherhill, 1996), pp. 46–47; Sōtōshū jinken yōgo suishin honbu, eds., "Uchiyama Gudō shi no meiyo kaifuku ni yosete," *Sōtōshū-hō,* no. 696, September 1993 (special supplement between p. 16 and p. 17).

[15] Kanzaki, *Taigyaku jiken soshō kiroku, shōko bussha,* vol. 8, p. 175.

[16] Letter to Ōishi Seinosuke of June 26, 1910; in Yoshida, *Nihon kindai bukkyōshi kenkyū,* p. 428.

[17] In Yoshida, *Nihon kindai bukkyōshi kenkyū,* pp. 435, 436.

[18] This book was not written by a subversive author but was in fact part of a history series in ten volumes, the *Dainippon jidaishi,* published by the academic press of Waseda University. Gudō owned the entire collection; see Morinaga, *Uchiyama Gudō,* pp. 102–103. Kume Kunitake (1839–1931) was one of the most influential historians of the time and a member of the Iwakura Mission to the West (1871–1873); see Wm. Theodore deBary, et al., eds., *Sources of Japanese Tradition* (abridged edition), 2 vols. (New York: Columbia University Press, 2006, second edition), vol. 2, tome 2, pp. 513–515; also pp. 15–16.

[19] Kemuyama Sentarō, *Kinsei museifushugi* (in *Meiji bunken shiryō sōsho, Shakaishugi hen,* vol. 3) (Tokyo: Meiji bunken, 1965); Kanzaki, *Taigyaku jiken soshō kiroku, shōko bussha,* vol. 1, pp. 43–45.

[20] Kashiwagi Ryūhō, *Uchiyama Gudō: Taigyaku jiken no ideorōgu* (Toki, Gifu Prefecture: Kaiko no sha, 1976), p. 50.

21 Letter to Ishikawa Sanshirō dated January 25, 1910; in Kashiwagi, *Uchiyama Gudō: Taigyaku jiken no ideorōgu*, p. 49.

22 Letter to Ishikawa of March 7, 1910; in Kashiwagi, *Uchiyama Gudō: Taigyaku jiken no ideorōgu*, p. 50.

23 These letters are included in Kashiwagi Ryūhō, *Taigyaku jiken to Uchiyama Gudō*, pp. 225–259; for an anthology, see Kashiwagi, *Uchiyama Gudō: Taigyaku jiken no ideorōgu*, pp. 36–55.

24 Ōsugi Sakae, a leading socialist/anarchist in Japan, studied foreign languages (principally French) at the Tokyo Foreign Languages School.

25 Ōsawa Masamichi, *Ōsugi Sakae kenkyū* (Tokyo: Hōsei Daigaku shuppan-kyoku, 1971), p. 45; quoted in Morinaga, *Uchiyama Gudō*, p. 143.

26 From Kinoshita's *Sensō no uta* (*War Songs*), published in *Heimin shinbun*, no. 31 (June 12, 1904) as part of the pacifist campaign against the Russo-Japanese War organized by the socialist organizations.

27 A different printing carries the cover title "Kitarubeki kakumei wa Museifu kyōsan" ("The Imminent Revolution is Anarchist-Communism"); Kanzaki, *Taigyaku jiken soshō kiroku, shōko bussha*, vol. 2, pp. 56–57; *Shakaishugi enkaku*, vol. 1, pp. 70, 262.

28 Morinaga, *Uchiyama Gudō*, p. 142.

29 A contextualization of ideas and movements against the imperial system can be found in Kanō Mikiyo and Amano Yasukazu, eds., *Han-tennōsei: "Hiko-kumin," "Taigyaku," Futei" no shisō* (Tokyo: Shakai hyōronsha, 1990).

30 This manuscript was not kept by the prison authorities but was returned in-stead to Gudō's relatives: Kanzaki, *Taigyaku jiken soshō kiroku, shōko bussha*, vol. 4, pp. 218–219.

31 Morinaga, *Uchiyama Gudō*, p. 110.

32 Yoshida, *Nihon kindai bukkyōshi kenkyū*, p. 435.

33 On this text, see Shirai Shinpei, *Anākizumu to tennōsei* (Tokyo: San'ichi Shobō, 1980), pp. 179–197. Shirai calls this manuscript a "paper bomb" (*kami no baku-dan*) (p. 196).

Chapter 2

1 On Sada Kaiseki, see Fabio Rambelli, "Sada Kaiseki: An Alternative Dis-course on Buddhism, Modernity, and Nationalism in the Early Meiji Period," in Roy Starrs, ed., *Politics and Religion in Japan: Red Sun, White Lotus* (London: Palgrave MacMillan, 2011), pp. 104–142.

2 The *Communist Manifesto* was translated into Japan by Kōtoku Shūsui and Sakai Tohihiko and published in *Heimin shinbun*, no. 53 (November 13, 1904) as *Kyōsantō sengen*.

3   On the origins of the Japanese socialist movement, see Crump, *The Origins of Socialist Thought in Japan;* on Kōtoku and his activities, including his relations with Gudō, see Notehelfer, *Kōtoku Shūsui: Portrait of a Japanese Radical;* on the history of anarchism in Japan, see Ōsawa Masamichi, *Anākizumu shisōshi: jiyū to hankō no ayumi* (Tokyo: Gendai Shichōsha, 1966), Akiyama Kiyoshi, *Nihon no hangyaku shisō* (Tokyo: Gendai shichōsha, 1968), and Komatsu Ryūji, *Nihon anākizumu undōshi* (Tokyo: Aoki shoten, 1972); for a brief survey in English, see Peter H. Marshall, *Demanding the Impossible: A History of Anarchism* (London: HarperCollins, 1992), pp. 523–527. On anarchism in general, see among others, George Woodcock, *Anarchism: A History of Libertarian Ideas and Movements* (Cleveland: Meridian Books, 1962); Marshall, *Demanding the Impossible: A History of Anarchism;* Paul McLaughlin, *Anarchism and Authority: A Philosophical Introduction to Classical Anarchism* (Aldershot, England, and Burlington, VT: Ashgate, 2007). For an interesting anthology of early Japanese writings about socialism, communism, and anarchism, see Yamaizumi Susumu, ed., *Shakaishugi kotohajime: Meiji ni okeru chokuyaku to jisei* (Tokyo: Shakai hyōronsha, 1990); in English, see de Bary, et al., eds., *Sources of Japanese Tradition,* vol. 2, tome 2, pp. 212–259. For an anthology of early Japanese anarchist writings, see Ōsawa Masamichi, ed., *Domin no shisō: Taishū no naka no anākizumu* (Tokyo: Shakai hyōronsha, 1990).

4   *Heimin shinbun,* no. 10 (January 17, 1904); in Morinaga, *Uchiyama Gudō,* p. 77. As a side note, it is interesting that Gudō's citations of the scriptures are incorrect, perhaps due to his lack of familiarity with *kanbun* (the form of Chinese language in which they are written).

5   *Da bannieban jing* (Jp. *Daihatsu nehangyō*), T.12.374:402c and passim.

6   Among them we find the infamous "discriminative posthumous names" or *sabetsu kamiyō,* in which certain groups of people belonging to the *hinin* (lit., "non-humans") and *eta* ("heavily defiled ones"), Japanese versions of the Indian *caṇḍāla* outcastes, were given Buddhist names that included expressions such as "slave" (*boku*) and "beast" (*chiku*). See William Bodiford, "Zen and the Art of Religious Prejudice," *Japanese Journal of Religious Studies* 23 (1–2) (1996): 1–27. See also the discussions of Critical Buddhism in Jamie Hubbard and Paul Swanson, eds., *Pruning the Bodhi Tree: The Storm Over Critical Buddhism* (Honolulu: University of Hawai'i Press, 1997).

7   *Jinggang banruo bolomituo jing* (Jp. *Kongō hannya haramitta kyō*), T.8.235:751c.

8   *Miaofa lianhua jing* (Jp. *Myōhō rengekyō;* also called *Fahua jing,* Jp. *Hokkekyō*), T.9.262:14c and passim.

9   *Miaofa lianhua jing,* T.9.262:14c and passim.

10   On these aspects of Gudō's thought and activity, see Ishikawa Rikizan, "Yōroppa bunka no ryūnyū to sono eikyō," *Sōtōshū sensho* 6 (1982): 68; Yoshida, *Nihon kindai bukkyōshi kenkyū,* p. 405.

11   Quoted in Morinaga, *Uchiyama Gudō,* p. 89.

[12] Rebecca Solnit, in *A Paradise Built in Hell* (New York: Penguin Books, 2009), has presented a powerful account of the importance of mutual aid and disinterested action during natural disasters, with explicit reference to anarchist thinkers.

[13] *Heibon no jikaku*, pp. 260, 263.

[14] *Muga no ai*, no. 13 (December 10, 1905); quoted in Kashiwagi Ryūhō, *Taigyaku jiken to Uchiyama Gudō*, p. 230; Morinaga, *Uchiyama Gudō*, p. 92.

[15] *Heimin shinbun*, no. 55 (September 18, 1904), as quoted in Morinaga, *Uchiyama Gudō*, pp. 68–69.

[16] In Kashiwagi, *Taigyaku jiken to Uchiyama Gudō*, p. 230; Morinaga, *Uchiyama Gudō*, p. 92. "Vast and long tongue" (*kōchōzetsu*) is a scriptural reference to the truthful and sincere words spoken by the Buddha; in this context, it also hints at the Zen idea of *mujō seppō:* "the nonsentient (i.e., nature) preaches the Dharma"; on the latter concept, see Fabio Rambelli, *Buddhist Materiality: A Cultural History of Objects in Japanese Buddhism* (Palo Alto, CA: Stanford University Press, 2007), pp. 48, 135, and passim.

[17] *Heimin shinbun*, no. 12 (January 31, 1904); in Morinaga, *Uchiyama Gudō*, p. 78.

[18] Morinaga, *Uchiyama Gudō*, p. 79.

[19] *Heibon no jikaku*, p. 268.

[20] *Heibon no jikaku*, p. 272.

[21] Among other leading anarchists of aristocratic descent, we find Mikhail Bakunin (1814–1876) and the Italian Carlo Cafiero (1846–1892).

[22] The most famous Japanese example, however, is certainly that of author Arishima Takeo (1878–1923), who in 1922, inspired by socialist ideas, gave up ownership of his large farm in Hokkaido in order to prepare himself for the coming revolution.

[23] Yano Fumio, *Shinshakai* (Tokyo: Dainippon tosho, 1902), p. 14; in Crump, *The Origins of Socialist Thought in Japan*, pp. 134–135.

[24] Kōtoku Shūsui, in his "Shakaishugi to kokutai"; quoted in Crump, *The Origins of Socialist Thought in Japan*, pp. 133–134. Analogous ideas of a monarchical-inspired socialism were widespread in Japan at the time; see for example Isoh Abé (Abé Isoo), "Socialism in Japan," in Shigénobu Okuma, ed., *Fifty Years of New Japan* (New York: Kraus, 1970, reprint), vol. 2, pp. 494–497.

[25] Crump, *The Origins of Socialist Thought in Japan*, p. 135. Predictably, Crump writes that this cannot properly be considered socialism. Ironically, the Nabeshima House is known for having handed down the set of samurai rules known as Hagakure, which were much praised by the writer and right-wing cultural critic Mishima Yukio; see Kathryn N. Sparling, trans., *The Way of the Samurai: Yukio Mishima on Hagakure in Modern Life* (New York: Basic Books, 1977).

[26] Morinaga, *Uchiyama Gudō*, pp. 36–37.

[27] Morinaga, *Uchiyama Gudō*, pp. 38–39.

[28] Morinaga, *Uchiyama Gudō*, p. 36.

[29] *Heimin shinbun*, no. 55 (September 18, 1904); in Morinaga, *Uchiyama Gudō*, pp. 68–69.

[30] Quoted in Morinaga, *Uchiyama Gudō*, p. 74. Authors have referred to this statement to argue whether or not Gudō himself had actually traveled to China. Morinaga is more cautious about this aspect of Gudō's life; see *Uchiyama Gudō*, p. 43.

[31] On Chinese temple life in the first half of the twentieth century, see Holmes Welch, *The Practice of Chinese Buddhism: 1900–1950* (Cambridge, MA: Harvard University Press, 1967).

[32] See Steven Collins, *Nirvana and Other Buddhist Felicities* (Cambridge: Cambridge University Press, 1998), esp. pp. 414–498.

[33] *Aggañña Sutta*, in Steven Collins, "The Discourse on What is Primary (*Aggañña-Sutta*): An Annotated Translation," *Journal of Indian Philosophy* 21 (4) (1993): 301–393. The Chinese version is *Xiaoyuan jing* (Jp. *Shōengyō*), in *Zhong Ahan jing* (Jp. *Chō Agonkyō*), T.1.1:36–39.

[34] See Sukumar Dutt, *Buddhist Monks and Monasteries of India* (London: George Allen and Unwin, 1962); J. P. Sharma, *Republics in Ancient India* (Leiden: E. J. Brill, 1968); Fabio Rambelli, "'Just Behave as You Like': Radical Amida Cults and Popular Religiosity in Premodern Japan," in Richard K. Payne and Kenneth K. Tanaka, eds., *Approaching the Land of Bliss: Religious Praxis in the Cult of Amitābha* (Honolulu: University of Hawai'i Press, 2004), pp. 169–201; and "Buddhist Republican Thought and Institutions in Japan: Preliminary Considerations," in *Japanese Studies Around the World 2008*, Special Issue "Scholars of Buddhism in Japan: Buddhist Studies in the 21st Century" (Kyoto: International Research Center for Japanese Studies, 2009), pp. 127–153. The existence of a "strong libertarian spirit" in Buddhism, especially the Zen tradition, has been emphasized by Marshall, *Demanding the Impossible: A History of Anarchism*, p. 65, but the brief chapter on Daoism and Buddhism (pp. 53–65) fails to do justice to either tradition.

[35] On the latter, see Rambelli, "'Just Behave as You Like': Radical Amida Cults and Popular Religiosity in Premodern Japan."

[36] See Michel Foucault, "Of Other Spaces" (1967), http://foucault.info/documents/heteroTopia/foucault.heteroTopia.en.html; accessed on March 3, 2013.

[37] *Heibon no jikaku*, p. 258.

[38] *Heibon no jikaku*, p. 265.

[39] *Heibon no jikaku*, p. 259.

40 *Heibon no jikaku*, p. 272.

41 *Heibon no jikaku*, p. 273.

42 *Heibon no jikaku*, p. 273.

43 *Heibon no jikaku*, p. 273.

44 On the relations between anarchism and Christianity from a more general perspective, see Jacques Ellul, *Anarchy and Christianity* (Grand Rapids, MI: W. B. Eerdmans, 1991).

45 Kashiwagi, *Taigyaku jiken to Uchiyama Gudō*, p. 239; Morinaga, *Uchiyama Gudō*, p. 106.

46 The image of the hand holding both an *ojuzu* (Buddhist rosary) and a bomb is particularly powerful and disturbing. It is interesting that we encounter similar, but less original, rhetoric in Buddhist wartime propaganda about the "sword that gives life." In *Zen and Japanese Culture* (Princeton, NJ: Princeton University Press, 1959), D. T. Suzuki writes: "The art of swordmanship distinguishes between the sword that kills and the sword that gives life. . . . the enemy appears and makes himself a victim . . . the word performs automatically its function of justice, which is the function of mercy" (p. 145).

   Nonetheless violence is certainly a complex issue for anarchism. A present-day Milanese anarchist in Italy said recently: "I don't feel I have been violent when I attack the symbols of man's power upon other men" (quoted in the Italian newsmagazine *L'Espresso*, July 19, 2012, p. 85). This echoes the passage in Gudō's pamphlet *Museifushugi Dōtoku hininron*, which emphasizes the intrinsic violent nature of state power, "Anarchism is a revolt against violent attacks targeting peaceful individuals."

47 This very controversial concept in East Asian Buddhism is apparently based on a particular interpretation of a passage in the *Yuqie shidi lun* (T.30:517b). For a discussion, see Harada Kōdō, "Butsugyō to zaisō," *Komazawa Daigaku bukkyō gakubu ronsō* 17 (1986): 125–142, especially pp. 133–136. This idea was also employed in the first half of the twentieth century by Buddhist apologists of Japanese imperialist warfare; see Victoria, *Zen at War*, pp. 87, 167.

48 For discussions of Buddhist attitudes toward violence, and war in particular, see, among others, Tessa J. Bartholomeusz, *In Defense of Dharma: Just War Ideology in Buddhist Sri Lanka* (London and New York: RoutledgeCurzon, 2002); Michael Jerryson and Mark Juergensmeyer, eds., *Buddhist Warfare* (Oxford and New York: Oxford University Press, 2010); Charles F. Keyes, "Political Crisis and Militant Buddhism," in Bardwell L. Smith, ed., *Religion and Legitimation of Power in Thailand, Laos, and Burma* (Chambersburg, PA: Anima, 1978), pp. 147–164; Lambert L. Schmithausen, "Aspects of the Buddhist Attitude Towards War," in Jan E. M. Houben and Karel L. van Kooij, eds., *Violence Denied* (Leiden and Boston: Brill, 1999), pp. 45–67; Stanley J. Tambiah, *Buddhism Betrayed? Religion, Politics, and Violence in Sri Lanka* (Chicago: University of Chicago Press, 1992).

[49] Quoted in Morinaga, *Uchiyama Gudō*, p. 104.

[50] In Kashiwagi, *Uchiyama Gudō: Taigyaku jiken no ideorōgu*, pp. 39–40.

[51] Morinaga, *Uchiyama Gudō*, pp. 123–124; Kanzaki, *Taigyaku jiken soshō kiroku, shōko bussha*, vol. 8, p. 177.

[52] Kindai Nihon shiryō kenkyūkai, eds., *Shakaishugisha enkaku* (Tokyo: Meiji bunken shiryō kankōkai, 1956), vol. 3, pp. 498–499.

[53] Morinaga, *Uchiyama Gudō*, p. 215; Kanzaki, *Taigyaku jiken soshō kiroku, shōko bussha*, vol. 8, p. 176.

[54] September 26, 1910; in Morinaga, *Uchiyama Gudō*, p. 214.

[55] September 30, 1910; in Morinaga, *Uchiyama Gudō*, p. 215.

[56] Morinaga, *Uchiyama Gudō*, p. 215.

[57] September 26, 1910; in Morinaga, *Uchiyama Gudō*, p. 214.

[58] Ninomiya Sontoku, also known as the "Peasant Sage of Japan," was an earlier promoter of agrarian reform and cooperative planning in the Odawara area, not far from Gudō's own temple. His emphasis on manual labor, cooperative activity, sincerity, and care for others (*magokoro*) strongly remind one of Gudō's own system of values. On Sontoku in English, see deBary, et al., eds., *Sources of Japanese Tradition*, pp. 475–483; Tadasu Yoshimoto, *A Peasant Sage of Japan: The Life and Work of Sontoku Ninomiya* (London: Longman's, Green and Co., 1912). On cooperative action in premodern Japan, see also Tetsuo Najita, *Ordinary Economies in Japan: A Historical Perspective, 1750–1950* (Berkeley: University of California Press, 2009).

[59] See Yoshida, *Nihon kindai bukkyō shakaishi kenkyū*, vol. 1, pp. 279–283; vol. 2, pp. 27–29; Yoshida also writes that Gudō's "reason" (*risei*) is very practical, not abstract, like in Zen, and ties up well with the iconoclastic and anti-authoritarian attitude of Zen, exemplified by expressions such as "he who does not work does not eat" and "Śākyamuni? Who is Śākyamuni?": Yoshida, *Nihon kindai bukkyō shakaishi kenkyū*, vol. 2, pp. 27–29. See also Morinaga, *Uchiyama Gudō*, p. 146.

[60] *Heibon no jikaku*, p. 272.

[61] Kanzaki, *Taigyaku jiken soshō kiroku, shōko bussha*, vol. 8, pp. 178, 179.

[62] Incidentally, we might notice that Diogenes of Sinope (412 or 404–323 B.C.E.) is sometimes indicated as one of the forerunners of modern anarchism.

Chapter 3

[1] Katō Hiroyuki, *Shinsei taii*, in Uete Michiari, ed., *Nishi Amane, Katō Hiroyuki* (Nihon no meicho, vol. 34) (Tokyo: Chūō kōronsha, 1972), p. 370.

[2] Komatsu, *Nihon anākizumu undōshi*, p. 23.

3   See Crump, *The Origins of Socialist Thought in Japan*, p. 39; Itoya Toshio, *Nihon shakaishugi undō shisōshi*, vol. 1 (Tokyo: Hōsei Daigaku shuppankyoku, 1979), p. 15.

4   See Peter (Piotr) Kropotkin, *The Conquest of Bread and Other Writings* (Cambridge: Cambridge University Press, 1995).

5   Morinaga, *Uchiyama Gudō*, pp. 148, 149.

6   Ōsawa Masamichi, "Anākizumu to shisō no dochaku: Taigyaku jiken ni renza shita sannin no sōryo," in Nakamura Yūjirō, ed., *Shisōshi no hōhō to kadai* (Tokyo: Tōkyō Daigaku shuppankai, 1973), pp. 397–398.

7   Sueki Fumihiko, *Meiji shisōka ron. Kindai Nihon no shisō saikō*, vol. 1 (Tokyo: Toransubyū, 2004), especially pp. 256–265.

8   Gudō's works repeat this term several times: the conscious family as "a little paradise" (*Heibon no jikaku*, p. 265); "our project to build a paradise" (p. 271), "all human beings must secure their clothing and food through their own labor—this is what the old sages called paradise (*tengoku*) or land of the gods (*shinkoku*)" and "realize as soon as possible such paradise" (p. 272); "factories should turn into collective properties of all the workers, thereby realizing democracy in the industrial sector; this is the first step toward the realization of paradise"; the "wholesome worker, ready to die in the struggle for paradise" (p. 273); "paradise of happiness" (p. 275).

9   See in particular Ōsawa, who focuses on Gudō's reference to the "holy spirit" in *Heibon no jikaku* (Ōsawa, "Anākizumu to shisō no dochaku: Taigyaku jiken ni renza shita sannin no sōryo," p. 393). References to Christianity in Gudō's writings include the parable of the grain of wheat, from the New Testament (John 12:24) (*Heibon no jikaku*, p. 273); "the light of freedom will doubtlessly and without fail illuminate one day the whole family and bestow its blessings upon all" (*Heibon no jikaku*, p. 266); the vision of an "eternal life (*eisei*)" (*Heibon no jikaku*, p. 273) as opposed to the path to extinction (*horobi*), the destiny of those who don't achieve consciousness or refuse to act accordingly; such an eternal life is characterized by happiness and is achieved through "enter[ing] the realm of consciousness" (*Heibon no jikaku*, p. 275); the idea that the "wholesome worker, ready to die in the struggle for paradise, is the person most loved by god" (*Heibon no jikaku*, p. 273); the idea that "capitalists and the classes in power" have committed "sins" they should repent (*Heibon no jikaku*, p. 273); and a direct reference to Jesus Christ (*Gokuchū shuki*, p. 279).

10 The French philosopher Ernest Renan (1823–1892) was perhaps the first to call Jesus and anarchist in his *Vie de Jesus* (1863): "Jesus, in some respects, was an anarchist, for he had no idea of a civil government. That government seemed to him purely and simply an abuse.... Every magistrate appeared to him a natural enemy of the people of god.... He wishes to annihilate riches and power, but not to appropriate them" (English translation in *The Life of Jesus* [London: Trübner and Co., 1864], pp. 112–113). Renan employs the term "anarchist" to indicate a naive idealist, and it is thus not an endorsement of

political anarchism. For a general treatment of the messianic ideas of socialism, see for instance Leszek Kolakowski, *Main Currents of Marxism* (New York and London: W. W. Norton, 2005). Ōsawa has already pointed to the fact that in Japan authors in the early twentieth century indicated affinities between Buddhism and socialism/anarchism (Ōsawa, "Anākizumu to shisō no dochaku: Taigyaku jiken ni renza shita sannin no sōryo," p. 375). Particularly notable in this respect is Kutsumi Kesson (1860–1925), who wrote that "in their spirit, Confucius, Śākaymuni, and Christ were all anarchists" (Kutsumi, *Museifushugi* [Tokyo: Heimin shobō, 1906], p. 3).

[11] On the complex relations between classical anarchism and religion, see Harold Barclay, "Anarchist Confrontations with Religion," in Jun and Wahl, eds., *New Perspectives on Anarchism*, pp. 169–185.

[12] On Eejanaika, see Fujitani Toshio, *Okagemairi to Eejanaika* (Tokyo: Iwanami shoten, 1968).

[13] On State Shinto, see Helen Hardacre, *Shinto and the State (1868–1945)* (Princeton, NJ: Princeton University Press, 1989).

[14] *Museifu kyōsan kakumei*, p. 252.

[15] *Museifu kyōsan kakumei*, p. 253.

[16] *Museifu kyōsan kakumei*, p. 253.

[17] *Heibon no jikaku*, p. 272.

[18] Kōtoku explicitly assimilated anarchism with philosophical Daoism, arguing that "the 'theory' of anarchism is virtually the same kind of philosophy as the East's Laozi and Zhuangzi" (quoted in Germaine A. Hoston, *The State, Identity, and the National Question in China and Japan* [Princeton, NJ: Princeton University Press, 1994], p. 143). In fact, Kōtoku took his pseudonym Shūsui (lit., "autumn water") from a passage from Zhuangzi ("The time of the autumn floods came. . . ."); Crump, *The Origins of Socialist Thought in Japan*, p. 128. See Burton Watson's translation, *Zhuangzi: Basic Writings* (New York: Columbia University Press, 2003), p. 97. On the anarchist components of Daoism, see John A. Rapp, "Daoism as Utopian or Accomodationist: Radical Daoism Re-examined in Light of the Guodian Manuscripts," in Laurence Davis and Ruth Kinna, eds., *Anarchism and Utopianism* (Manchester and New York: Manchester University Press, 2009), pp. 33–52.

[19] Murray N. Rothbard, "Concepts of the Role of Intellectuals in Social Change Toward Laissez Faire," *The Journal of Libertarian Studies* 9 (2), (Fall 1990): 46.

[20] *Sekai fujin*, no. 21 (January 1, 1908); in Morinaga, *Uchiyama Gudō*, p. 106.

[21] On this, see also the pamphlet he published entitled *Museifu kyōsan dōtoku hinin*.

[22] Citations from the *Analects of Confucius*; see respectively, Raymond Dawson,

trans., *Confucius: The Analects* (Oxford and New York: Oxford University Press, 1993), pp. 61, 14; in *Heibon no jikaku*, pp. 260, 273.

23 Sakura Sōgorō, a village headman in Kanto region, appealed directly to the shogun, Tokugawa Yoshitsuna, against the oppressive governance of his feudal lord, Hotta Masanobu; his request was eventually granted, but he, his wife, and his four male sons were executed and his tomb later became a sacred site for villagers in the Sakura district; see Anne Walthall, *Peasant Uprisings in Japan* (Chicago and London: University of Chicago Press, 1991), pp. 35–75. Ōshio Heihachirō was a magistrate in Osaka at the time of a grave famine; indignant about the government's lack of concern for the thousands of people affected, he organized a revolt and attacked the residences of the city administrators and wealthy merchants; the revolt failed and all its participants, including Ōshio and his son, committed suicide; see deBary, et al., eds., *Sources of Japanese Tradition*, pp. 467–475; Ivan Morris, *The Nobility of Failure: Tragic Heroes in the History of Japan* (New York: The Noonday Press, 1975), pp. 180–216.

24 On this, see of course Morris, *The Nobility of Failure: Tragic Heroes in the History of Japan*.

25 On this, see Crump, *The Origins of Socialist Thought in Japan*, p. 124.

26 For a preliminary study on the impact of the French Revolution in Japan, see Kobayashi Yoshiaki, *Meiji Ishin to Furansu kakumei* (Tokyo: San'ichi shobō, 1988).

27 On this subject, see Umberto Eco, *Il superuomo di massa* (Milan: Bompiani, 1976).

28 We should also recall that Kōtoku Shūsui, who was so influential in Gudō's intellectual and political formation, had studied with philosopher and politician Nakae Chōmin (1847–1901).

29 Hoston, *The State, Identity, and the National Question in China and Japan*, p. 138.

30 Hoston, *The State, Identity, and the National Question in China and Japan*, p. 139.

"*Vademecum* for the Soldiers in the Imperial Army"

1 This is a reference to the French economist of classical liberal ideas, Jean Baptiste Say (1767–1832).

2 This is the "Song of the Conscripts" from *War Songs (Sensō no Uta)* by Kinoshita Naoe; see Chapter 1, n. 26.

"Anarchism and the Repudiation of Morals"

1 These three sentences that open the pamphlet, together with the six sentences that conclude it, are not in the original text by Baginsky and appear to have been added by Gudō.

"Anarchist Communist Revolution"

1   All of these are famous tourist resorts; in Gudō's time they were also areas in which the upper classes in the Tokyo region had vacation homes.

2   *O-bon* is the midsummer festival that takes place on August 15.

3   This revolutionary "song" is Uchiyama's variation on a popular socialist song, "Shakaitō rappabushi" ("Fanfare of the Socialist Party"), first published in a socialist magazine in 1906; see Morinaga, *Uchiyama Gudō*, p. 131.

4   According to the *Nihon shoki* (720 C.E.), an ancient Japanese mytho-historical text, the tribal leader Nagasunebiko organized the resistance against Emperor Jinmu's conquest of the Kumano area, but was eventually killed by a god of the imperial clan; see W. G. Aston, trans., *Nihongi: Chronicles of Japan from the Earliest Times to A.D. 697* (Tokyo: Tuttle, 1972), pp. 113, 126–128.

5   Kumasaka Chōhan, a character in medieval war hero Minamoto no Yoshitsune's cycle of stories, became a synonym for a great thief; Shuten Dōji is a terrible monster and brigand of popular legend.

6   The text has *ban'ei*, probably a misspelling for *banpei* (guards); I have modified my translation accordingly.

7   Indicated as Kimura Genjirō in Gudō's text.

6   Also known as Ogure Reiko.

"Common Consciousness"

1   For "fraternity" the text has *hakuai*, lit., humanitarianism or philanthropy. This is an obvious reference to "freedom, equality, and fraternity" (*liberté, égalité, fraternité*), the slogan of the 1789 French Revolution.

2   This proverb suggests that things that are apparently useless or harmful can be put to good use.

3   This is an incorrect citation of a sentence from the *Analects of Confucius*, which reads instead *mi wo koroshite jin wo nasu*, "sacrifice yourself in order to realize the virtue of humaneness." The full quote is: "The determined public servant and the humane man never seek to preserve life in such a way as to injure humaneness, but they will sometimes even sacrifice their lives in order to achieve humaneness" (Dawson, trans., *Confucius: The Analects*, p. 61).

4   One *sen* is one cent of a yen in the old denomination.

5   From 1888 until 1926, the electorate for local councils was divided into first and second classes on the basis of personal wealth and amount of taxes paid. First-class electors were the wealthiest members of the community and even though their numbers were very small, they had the right to elect one half of the members of local councils. The other half was chosen by the larger group of second-class electors.

6   This section follows "Municipal Consciousness" but is listed before the latter in the list of sections given at the beginning of the text.

7   A quote from the *Analects* (Dawson, trans., *Confucius: The Analects*, p. 14).

8   This is a quote from the New Testament (John 12:24). It means that a grain of wheat will be able to bear fruit, and thus fulfill its mission, only if it falls into the ground and "dies"; if it doesn't, it will be just a minuscule grain of wheat. This passage of the Gospel is normally interpreted as a metaphor of Jesus' own death and resurrection. Gudō interprets it as a symbol of exemplary revolutionary self-sacrifice.

9   A *tsubo* is a plot of land that corresponds to approximately 3.30 square meters or 35 square feet.

10   This is perhaps a reference to the prison in Abashiri, in northern Hokkaidō, where several political prisoners were imprisoned.

References

Primary Sources

T   *Taishō shinshū daizōkyō*, 85 vols. Takakusu Junjirō and Watanabe
     Kaigyoku, eds. Tokyo: Issaikyō kankōkai, 1924–1932.

UG   "Uchiyama Gudō shū," in *Sōtōshū sensho*, vol. 6. Kyōgihen, Tai gairai shisō.
     Edited by Hideo Sakurai. General supervision by Genryū Kagamishima
     and Hideo Sakurai. Kyoto: Dōhōsha shuppan, 1982.

Works by Uchiyama Gudō

Museifu kyōsan kakumei (Nyūgoku kinen), in "Uchiyama Gudō shū," pp. 245–256.

Heibon no jikaku, in "Uchiyama Gudō shū," pp. 256–275.

Gokuchū shuki, in "Uchiyama Gudō shū," pp. 276–280.

Texts Published by Ushiyama Gudō (translated by others)

Teikoku gunjin zayū no mei, in "Uchiyama Gudō shū," pp. 281–284.

Museifushugi dōtoku hininron, in "Uchiyama Gudō shū," pp. 284–292.

Buddhist Scriptures

Da bannieban jing (*Great Nirvana Sutra*; Skt. *Mahāparinirvāṇa-sūtra*; Jp. *Daihatsu nehangyō*), T.12.374.

Jinggang banruo bolomituo jing (*Diamond Sutra*; Skt. *Vajracchedikāprajñāpāramitā-sūtra*; Jp. *Kongō hannya haramitta kyō*), T.8.235.

Miaofa lianhua jing (*Lotus Sutra*; Skt. *Saddharmapuṇḍarīka-sūtra*; Jp. *Myōhō renge kyō*; also called *Fahua jing*, Jp. *Hokkekyō*), T.9.262.

Xiaoyuan jing (Jp. *Shōengyō*), in *Zhong Ahan jing* (Jp. *Chō Agonkyō*), T.1.1:36–39).

Yuqie shidi lun (Skt. *Yogācārabhūmi-śāstra*, Jp. *Yuga shiji ron*), T.30.1579.

Secondary Sources

Abé, Isoh (Abe Isoo). "Socialism in Japan," in Shigénobu Ōkuma, ed., *Fifty Years of New Japan*, vol. 2, pp. 494–512. New York: Kraus, 1970, reprint. Original edition, London 1910.

Akiyama Kiyoshi. *Nihon no hangyaku shisō*. Tokyo: Gendai shichōsha, 1968.

Anderson, Benedict R. *Under Three Flags: Anarchism and the Anti-colonial Imagination*. London and New York: Verso, 2005.

Anonymous. *"Aux conscripts," L'anarchie*, September 27, 1906, p. 4.

Aston, W. G., trans. *Nihongi: Chronicles of Japan from the Earliest Times to A.D. 697*. Tokyo: Tuttle, 1972. Original edition, 1896.

Asukai Masamichi, ed. *Kōtoku Shūsui shū*. *Kindai Nihon shisō taikei*, vol. 13. Tokyo: Chikuma shobō, 1975.

Baginski, Max. "Anti-Moral Reflections," *Mother Earth* 2 (6) (August 1907): 246–249.

Barclay, Harold. "Anarchist Confrontations with Religion," in Nathan J. Jun and Shane Wahl, eds., *New Perspectives on Anarchism*, pp. 169–185. Lanham, MD: Lexington Books, 2010.

Bartholomeusz, Tessa J. *In Defense of Dharma: Just War Ideology in Buddhist Sri Lanka*. London and New York: RoutledgeCurzon, 2002.

Bodiford, William. "Zen and the Art of Religious Prejudice," *Japanese Journal of Religious Studies* 23 (1–2) (1996): 1–27.

Butterworth, Alex. *The World That Never Was: A True Story of Dreamers, Schemers, Anarchists & Secret Agents*. New York: Pantheon Books, 2010.

Chesneaux, Jean. "Egalitarian and Utopian Traditions in the East," *Diogenes* 16 (62) (1968): 76–102.

Collins, Steven. *Nirvana and Other Buddhist Felicities*. Cambridge: Cambridge University Press, 1998.

—."The Discourse on What is Primary (*Aggañña-Sutta*): An Annotated Translation," *Journal of Indian Philosophy* 21 (4) (1993): 301–393.

Crump. John. *The Origins of Socialist Thought in Japan*. London: Croom Helm; New York: St. Martin's Press, 1983.

Dawson, Raymond, trans. *Confucius: The Analects*. Oxford and New York: Oxford University Press, 1993.

deBary, Wm. Theodore, et al., eds. *Sources of Japanese Tradition, Abridged Edition*, 2 vols. New York: Columbia University Press, 2006, second edition.

Dutt, Sukumar. *Buddhist Monks and Monasteries of India*. London: George Allen and Unwin, 1962.

Eco, Umberto. *Il superuomo di massa*. Milan: Bompiani, 1976.

Ellul, Jacques. *Anarchy and Christianity*. Grand Rapids, MI: W. B. Eerdmans, 1991.

Enzesberger, Hans Magnus. *La breve estate dell'anarchia: vita e morte di Buenaventura Durruti*. Milan: Feltrinelli, 1973.

Foucault, Michel. "Of Other Spaces" (1967). http://foucault.info/documents/heteroTopia/foucault.heteroTopia.en.html.

Fujitani Toshio. *Okagemairi to eejanaika*. Tokyo: Iwanami shoten, 1968.

Harada Kōdō. "Butsugyō to zaisō," *Komazawa Daigaku bukkyō gakubu ronsō* 17 (1986): 125–142.

Hardacre, Helen. *Shinto and the State (1868–1945)*. Princeton, NJ: Princeton University Press, 1989.

Hoston, Germaine A. *The State, Identity, and the National Question in China and Japan*. Princeton, NJ: Princeton University Press, 1994.

Hubbard, Jamie, and Paul Swanson, eds. *Pruning the Bodhi Tree: The Storm Over Critical Buddhism.* Honolulu: University of Hawai'i Press, 1997.

Inagaki Masami. *Henkaku wo motometa bukkyōsha.* Tokyo: Daizō shuppan, 1975.

Ishikawa Rikizan. "The Social Response of Buddhists to the Modernization of Japan: The Contrasting Lives of Two Sōtō Zen Monks," *Japanese Journal of Religious Studies* 25 (1–2) (1998): 87–115.

—."Yōroppa bunka no ryūnyū to sono eikyō," *Sōtōshū sensho* 6 (1982): 461–470.

Itoya Toshio. *Nihon shakaishugi undō shisōshi,* vol. 1. Tokyo: Hōsei Daigaku shuppankyoku, 1979.

Jerryson, Michael, and Mark Juergensmeyer, eds. *Buddhist Warfare.* Oxford and New York: Oxford University Press, 2010.

Jun, Nathan J. *Anarchism and Political Modernity.* London and New York: Continuum, 2012.

Kanō Mikiyo, and Amano Yasukazu, eds. *Han-tennōsei: "Hikokumin," "Taigyaku," Futei" no shisō.* Series Shisō no umi he: Kaihō to henkaku, vol. 16. Tokyo: Shakai hyōronsha, 1990.

Kanzaki Kiyoshi, ed. *Kakumei densetsu taigyaku jiken,* 4 vols. Tokyo: Kodomo no miraisha, 2010.

—,ed. *Taigyaku jiken soshō kiroku, shōko bussha.* Tokyo: Kindai Nihon shiryō kenkyūkai, 1960–1962.

Kashiwagi Ryūhō. "Junkyōsha Uchiyama Gudo no shōgai," *Nishi-Sagami shomin shiroku* 9 (1984).

—,ed. *Taigyaku jiken no shūhen: Heiminsha chihō dōshi no hitobito.* Tokyo: Ronsōsha, 1980.

—.*Taigyaku jiken to Uchiyama Gudō.* Tokyo: JCA shuppan, 1979.

—.*Uchiyama Gudō: Taigyaku jiken no ideorōgu.* Toki, Gifu Prefecture: Kaiko no sha, 1976.

Katō Hiroyuki. "Shinsei taii," in Uete Michiari, ed., *Nishi Amane, Katō Hiroyuki,* pp. 345–379. Series Nihon no meicho, vol. 34. Tokyo: Chūō kōronsha, 1972.

Kemuyama Sentarō. *Kinsei museifushugi.* In *Meiji bunken shiryō sōsho, Shakaishugi hen,* vol. 3. Tokyo: Meiji bunken, 1965.

Keyes, Charles F. "Political Crisis and Militant Buddhism," in Bardwell L. Smith, ed., *Religion and Legitimation of Power in Thailand, Laos, and Burma,* pp. 147–164. Chambersburg, PA: Anima, 1978.

Kihara Minoru. *Ryōka no nagare: Waga kusawake no shakaishugisha-tachi.* Tokyo: Orijin shuppan sentā, 1977.

Kindai Nihon shiryō kenkyūkai, eds. *Shakaishugisha enkaku,* 3 vols. Tokyo: Meiji bunken shiryō kankōkai, 1956.

Kobayashi Yoshiaki. *Meiji Ishin to Furansu kakumei.* Tokyo: San'ichi shobō, 1988.

Kolakowski, Leszek. *Main Currents of Marxism.* New York and London: W. W. Norton, 2005.

Komatsu Ryūji. *Nihon anākizumu undōshi.* Tokyo: Aoki shoten, 1972.

References

References

References

References

Kropotkin, Peter (Piotr). *The Conquest of Bread and Other Writings.* Cambridge: Cambridge University Press, 1995, reprint. Original edition, 1982.

Kume Kunitake. *Nihon kodaishi.* Series Dainippon jidaishi. Tokyo: Waseda Daigaku shuppanbu, 1907.

Kutsumi Kesson. 1906. *Museifushugi.* Tokyo: Heimin shobō, 1906.

Marshall, Peter H. *Demanding the Impossible: A History of Anarchism.* London: HarperCollins, 1992.

McLaughlin, Paul. *Anarchism and Authority: A Philosophical Introduction to Classical Anarchism.* Aldershot, England, and Burlington, VT: Ashgate, 2007.

Morinaga Eizaburō. *Uchiyama Gudō.* Tokyo: Ronsōsha, 1984.

Morris, Ivan. *The Nobility of Failure: Tragic Heroes in the History of Japan.* New York: The Noonday Press, 1975.

Najita, Tetsuo. *Ordinary Economies in Japan: A Historical Perspective, 1750–1950.* Berkeley: University of California Press, 2009.

Notehelfer, F. G. *Kōtoku Shūsui: Portrait of a Japanese Radical.* London: Cambridge University Press, 1971.

Ōsawa Masamichi. *Anākizumu shisōshi: jiyū to hankō no ayumi.* Tokyo: Gendai Shichōsha, 1966.

—. "Anākizumu to shisō no dochaku: Taigyaku jiken ni renza shita sannin no sōryo," in Nakamura Yūjirō, ed., *Shisōshi no hōhō to kadai,* pp. 374–398. Tokyo: Tōkyō Daigaku shuppankai, 1973.

—, ed. *Domin no shisō: Taishū no naka no anākizumu.* Series Shisō no umi he: Kaihō to henkaku, vol. 17. Tokyo: Shakai hyōronsha, 1990.

—. *Ōsugi Sakae kenkyū.* Tokyo: Hōsei Daigaku shuppankyoku, 1971.

Pedrini, Riccardo. *Libera Baku ora.* Rome: DeriveApprodi, 2000.

Rambelli, Fabio. *Buddhist Materiality: A Cultural History of Objects in Japanese Buddhism.* Palo Alto, CA: Stanford University Press, 2007.

—. "Buddhist Republican Thought and Institutions in Japan: Preliminary Considerations," in *Japanese Studies Around the World 2008,* Special Issue "Scholars of Buddhism in Japan: Buddhist Studies in the 21st Century," pp. 127–153. Kyoto: International Research Center for Japanese Studies, 2009.

—. "'Just Behave as You Like': Radical Amida Cults and Popular Religiosity in Premodern Japan," in Richard K. Payne and Kenneth K. Tanaka, eds., *Approaching the Land of Bliss: Religious Praxis in the Cult of Amitābha,* pp. 169–201. Honolulu: University of Hawai'i Press, 2004.

—. "Sada Kaiseki: An Alternative Discourse on Buddhism, Modernity, and Nationalism in the Early Meiji Period," in Roy Starrs, ed., *Politics and Religion in Japan: Red Sun, White Lotus,* pp. 104–142. London: Palgrave MacMillan, 2011.

—. "'The Dharma Preaches Equality and Has No Hierarchy': Buddhism and the Anarcho-Communist Movement in Japan," in Patrice Ladwig, ed., *Buddhist Socialisms in Asia.* London and New York: Routledge, 2013.

Rapp, John A. "Daoism as Utopian or Accomodationist: Radical Daoism Re-examined in Light of the Guodian Manuscripts," in Laurence Davis and Ruth

Kinna, eds., *Anarchism and Utopianism*, pp. 33–52. Manchester and New York: Manchester University Press, 2009.

Renan, Ernest. *The Life of Jesus.* London: Trübner and Co., 1864.

Rothbard, Murray N. "Concepts of the Role of Intellectuals in Social Change Toward Laissez Faire," *The Journal of Libertarian Studies* 9 (2) (Fall 1990): 43–67.

Saki Ryūzō. *Shōsetsu Taigyaku Jiken.* Tokyo: Bungei shunjū, 2001.

Schmithausen, Lambert L. "Aspects of the Buddhist Attitude Towards War," in Jan E. M. Houben and Karel L. van Kooij, eds., *Violence Denied: Violence, Non-Violence, and the Rationalization of Violence in South Asian Cultural History,* pp. 45–67. Leiden and Boston: Brill, 1999.

Sekigawa, Natsuo, and Jirō Taniguchi. *Au temps de Botchan,* 5 vols. Paris: Seuil, 2005.

Shakaishugi enkaku, 2 vols. Series Zoku Gendaishi shiryō, vols. 1–2. Tokyo: Misuzu shobō, 1982.

Sharma, J. P. *Republics in Ancient India.* Leiden: E. J. Brill, 1968.

Shioda Shōhei and Watanabe Junzō, eds. *Hiroku Taigyaku jiken,* 2 vols. Tokyo: Shunjūsha, 1959.

Shirai Shinpei. *Anākizumu to tennōsei.* Tokyo: San'ichi Shobō, 1980.

Solnit, Rebecca. *A Paradise Built in Hell: The Extraordinary Communities That Arise in Disaster.* New York: Penguin Books, 2009.

Sōtōshū jinken yōgo suishin honbu, eds. "Uchiyama Gudō shi no meiyo kaifuku ni yosete," *Sōtōshū-hō,* no. 696, September 1993 (special supplement between pp. 16 and 17).

Sparling, Kathryn N., trans. *The Way of the Samurai: Yukio Mishima on Hagakure in Modern Life.* New York: Basic Books, 1977.

Sueki Fumihiko. *Meiji shisōka ron.* Kindai Nihon no shisō saikō, vol. 1. Tokyo: Toransubyū, 2004.

Suga Hidemi. *"Teikoku" no bungaku: sensō to "Taigyaku" no aida.* Tokyo: Ibunsha, 2001.

Suzuki, Daisetz T. *Zen and Japanese Culture.* Princeton, NJ: Princeton University Press, 1959.

Tambiah, Stanley J. *Buddhism Betrayed? Religion, Politics, and Violence in Sri Lanka.* Chicago: University of Chicago Press, 1992.

Tanaka Nobumasa. *Taigyaku jiken: Shi to sei no gunzō.* Tokyo: Iwanami shoten, 2010.

Victoria, Brian. *Zen at War.* New York and Tokyo: Weatherhill, 1996.

Walthall, Anne. *Peasant Uprisings in Japan.* Chicago and London: University of Chicago Press, 1991.

Watson, Burton, trans. *Zhuangzi: Basic Writings.* New York: Columbia University Press, 2003.

Welch, Holmes. *The Practice of Chinese Buddhism: 1900–1950.* Cambridge, MA: Harvard University Press, 1967.

Woodcock, George. Anarchism: *A History of Libertarian Ideas and Movements.* Cleveland: Meridian Books, 1962.

Yamaizumi Susumu, ed. *Shakaishugi kotohajime: Meiji ni okeru chokuyaku to jisei.* Series Shisō no umi he: Kaihō to henkaku, vol. 8. Tokyo: Shakai hyōronsha, 1990.

Yano Fumio. 1902. *Shinshakai.* Tokyo, Dainippon tosho.

Yoshida Kyūichi. *Nihon kindai bukkyō shakaishi kenkyū,* 2 vols., rev. ed., in *Yoshida Kyūichi chosakushū.* Tokyo: Kawashima shoten, 1991.

—.*Nihon kindai bukkyōshi kenkyū,* in *Yoshida Kyūichi chosakushū,* vol. 1. Tokyo: Kawashima shoten, 1992.

Yoshimoto, Tadasu. *A Peasant Sage of Japan: The Life and Work of Sontoku Ninomiya.* London: Longman's, Green and Co., 1912.

Index

Museifu kyōsan kakumei 無政府共産
革命 ("Anarchist Communist
Revolution"), xix, xx, xxi, xxii,
xxiv–xxv, xxvi–xxvii, 17–18
in *Sekai fujin* 世界婦人 (magazine),
33
utopias and utopian visions:
anarchist paradise, 9, 16, 18, 20–22
and enlightened rulers, 16, 21
socialism and messianic ideas,
91–92n10
tengoku 天国 (soteriological and eschatological image of paradise),
22, 31–32, 63, 91n8
See also new society (*shinshakai* 新社
会); soteriology
Utsunomiya Takuji 宇都宮卓爾, 51

"*Vademecum* for the Soldiers in the
Imperial Army" (*Teikoku gunjin
zayū no mei* 帝国軍人座右之銘),
6–7, 85n26
"Song of Conscripts" (by Kinoshita
Naoe 木下尚) quoted in, 7, 38,
85n26
translation of, 37–38
See also Ōsugi Sakae 大杉栄
Victoria, Brian, xiv, 84n14, 89n47
villagers' consciousness, 59–61
violence:
advocated by Gudō against revolutionary opponents, 62
contextualization of Gudō's calls
for, xxv, 4–5, 23–25
and direct action, 4–5, 23–26, 27, 51
image of a hand holding both an
ojuzu (Buddhist rosary) and a
bomb, xxiii, 24, 89n46
moral legitimacy of the use of, 24
progaganda as more effective than,
26
and revolutionary heroes, 34
and state power, xvii–xviii, 89n46
violent anarchism supported by

Gudō, xxv, 4–5, 8, 18, 24–26, 51,
89n46
between workers at dam construction site, 74
See also direct action; military; nonviolence; terrorism (*ansatsushugi*
暗殺主義); warfare

Wang Yangming 王陽明 (1472–1529),
33
warfare:
Buddhist attitudes toward, 24,
89nn46-47
as criminal endeavors benefiting
profiteers, 38, 74
state power as the source of, 18, 50
See also military service
Watanabe Kan'emon 渡辺勘右衛門
(landowner in Ōhiradai), 3, 16,
83n3
wealth disparity, 3, 9–10, 16, 59–60,
83n3
and Buddhist economics, xx
greed/exploitation as the root of,
17, 19–20, 59
and wealth redistribution, xi, 10, 60
See also capitalism; money
Wen 文 (Chinese king), 16
Western ideas:
about socialism related to Confucianism, 33–34
and the Allied Occupation, x–xi
European anarchist texts printed by
Gudō, ix
and the French Revolution, 34, 94n1
Iwakura Mission to the West, 84n18
radical socialist movement in the
United States (nineteenth century), 4, 83n6
social Darwinism, 14
See also Baginski, Max; Christianity;
Kropotkin, Peter (Piotr)
women:
and family responsibilities/raising
of, 18, 56, 58